Meet me at Mike's

26 crafty projects and things to make

Published in 2009
by Hardie Grant Books
85 High Street
Prahran, Victoria 3181, Australia
www.hardiegrant.com.au
www.hardiegrant.co.uk

Text copyright © Pip Lincolne 2009
Photographs copyright © Tim James 2009

A catalogue record for this book is available from the National Library of Australia.
ISBN: 978 1 74066 630 5

Designed by Simone Elder at Ortolan
Edited by Janine Flew
Printed and bound in China by C&C Offset Printing

3 5 7 9 10 8 6 4

The projects in this book are the original designs owned by the artists who created them.
Have fun making the projects, but please do not sell any of the things you make from this book.

Please note that some of the projects in this book have not been made for children
and may use components that could be harmful if swallowed.

In a world gone green, hand made makes sense.
It's more ethical, more authentic and more beautiful.
It's unique in its imperfection. And it's accessible.
Unlike the mass produced, craft inspires an urge to create.
That fantastic thought – 'I think I could make something like that' –
which fuels all sorts of wonderful beginnings involving fabric or glue.

Meet me at Mike's

26 crafty projects and
things to make

by PIP LINCOLNE

Hardie Grant Books

MELBOURNE · LONDON

Contents

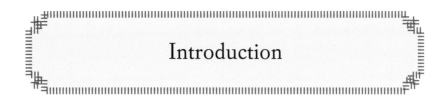

Introduction

Meet Me at Mike's is a sweet smile of a store on a busy street in a lovely city. And it belongs to lucky me! When I started Mike's, I wanted it to be something special. I wanted to do more than sell lovely hand-made things. I wanted to light up the whole neighbourhood with goodness too! I wanted to make people happy, share ideas and provide a meeting place for creative types. Above all, though, I really wanted to get people excited about their own crafty potential. Especially people that might not have realised how much fun it is to make stuff.

So, I started a blog, www.meetmeatmikes.com to share inspiration and encouragement, I started a craft group, www.brownowls.blogspot.com so we could all meet each other in real life and I decided to write this book, because some people don't like computers much, or they might be shy and I wanted to get those people crafting along with us too. In it you will find 26 projects created by myself and some crafty friends.

Making is one of life's great joys. The sweet simplicity of producing something with your own hands is pretty unbeatable. Especially when you weren't sure you could do it. You don't need lots of experience. You don't need to be an artist. You don't need to be standing in the line that says 'good with hands'. You most certainly don't need to spend lots of money or have heaps of equipment either.

You do need a sense of humour and a bit of persistence. I don't want to be too sunshiny, because sometimes things don't turn out as planned for the crafty novice, but navigate the choppy-yet-pretty seas of crafty know-how and I think you'll realise that sometimes things work just beautifully. And it is those beautiful moments that are worth their weight in gold.

My advice to you on your crafty voyage is:
Always read your instructions carefully before you start. Be sure you have all the equipment required – and the amount of time allocated – plus a bit more for popping to the shops for chocolate biscuits and things. Know your neighbour – someone you know may have hidden crafty talents to share! Phone a friend – it's always more fun to have someone to chat to. Don't get hung up on perfection. Practice really does make perfect. Above all, just dive in. Succeed or not. It doesn't matter – you can always try again and you've probably learnt something too!

Have a go. I dare you.

Pip Lincolne
xx

Dedicated to
my extra good daughter, Rin,
my mum and my nanna
who are very nice
and crafty too.

PROJECTS

Teeny-tiny goody-two-shoes

I love anything in miniature, and these gorgeous baby shoes are no exception. Reclaimed vintage embroidery makes each pair unique. If you don't have a baby in your life, make them anyway. They look perfectly lovely just perched on a shelf or framed in a little shadow box.

PROJECT BY: ALLISON JONES
SUITABLE FOR: BEGINNERS
SHOULD TAKE: ABOUT 2 HOURS THE FIRST TIME, QUICKER NEXT TIME!

SHOPPING LIST

◇ One vintage cotton tablecloth or a couple of vintage napkins or a pillowcase with a nice embroidered border (Fabric 1)
◇ 30 cm × 30 cm piece of printed cotton (Fabric 2)
◇ 30 cm of 6-mm wide elastic
◇ Matching thread

CRAFTY NEEDS

◇ Sewing machine
◇ Scissors
◇ Measuring tape or ruler
◇ Dressmaker's pins
◇ Iron
◇ Seam ripper in case of mistakes

PATTERN NEEDS

◇ There are three pattern pieces: sole of shoe, back of shoe and front of shoe.
◇ From Fabric 1, cut two front of shoe pieces (make sure these are positioned nicely on the embroidery, as this will be the front part of the shoe, where the toes go – make it super cute!).
◇ From Fabric 2, cut two front of shoe pieces.
◇ From Fabric 2, cut four back of shoe pieces.
◇ From Fabric 2, cut four sole of shoe pieces.

BEFORE YOU START SEWING

◇ Cut out the pattern pieces as detailed earlier.
◇ You will have 12 pieces in total, six for each shoe.
◇ Make sure your machine is threaded and your bobbin is full.
◇ Get a cup of tea and an Iced Vo Vo.
◇ You'll see lots of special symbols and letters on the patterns – they are there to help you match and sew all the tiny shoe pieces together correctly. Have a look at the pattern pieces and then read on! If you work carefully, your shoes will be just great the very first time.

1. Get to know the pattern and mark your pieces

Note where the markings are on the pattern pieces. You need to mark the sole at point A and point B. To do this, just put a tiny line on the right side of the fabric at the very edge (pen is fine). You also need to mark the front of shoe piece at points C and D. Also have a look to see where the triangle, heart, nought and cross symbols are marked on two of the pattern pieces. This sounds tricky, but it's really not – it's just to help you match up the curvy bits more easily.

2. Prepare your pieces

Separate your pieces into two piles, one for each shoe. Each pile should have one front of shoe front piece in Fabric 1, one front of shoe piece in Fabric 2, two back of shoe pieces in Fabric 2, and two sole of shoe pieces in Fabric 2.

Now put one pile to the side and we'll make one shoe at a time.

3. Sew the shoe front

Take the Fabric 1 (embroidered) shoe front piece and a Fabric 2 shoe front piece. With right sides facing, pin them together. Sew neatly, about 1 cm in from the edge, all the way along Seam C. Trim and clip the curved edge. Turn the piece right side out and press it flat.

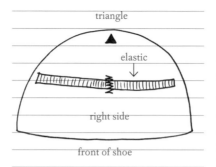

4. Attach the elastic to the shoe front

Cut a 15 cm piece of elastic. Fold it in half, mark the centre point with a pen, then pin this marked point to point F on the Fabric 2 side of the shoe front piece. Sew firmly in place with a short zig-zag stitch.

5. Sew the sole pieces

With wrong sides facing, pin together two sole pieces. Sew all around, 5 mm in from the edge, using a straight stitch. Then go over it with a zig-zag stitch (or an overlocker of you have one) even closer to the edge of the fabric to stop it fraying too much. (The raw edge doesn't need to be super neat, as no-one will see this seam.)

6. Sew the back of shoe pieces

With right sides facing, pin together the two back of shoe pieces. Sew neatly from point G to point H and on to points I and J. Trim any messy edges. Make sure that the shorter bottom edge is left open. Turn the piece right side out and press neatly.

7. Make the casing for the elastic to go through

Now take this back of shoe unit that you have just made and fold the long edge down 2 cm (as shown) to form a casing. Stitch a seam 1.5 cm down from the folded edge. This is where you will thread the elastic through later on.

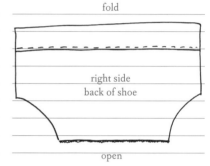

8. Sew it all together

Make sure you've clipped all the raw edges as neatly as possible. When sewing all the bits together, take your time and have the machine on the slowest speed, as you need to ease the pieces together as you sew them into a curved shape.

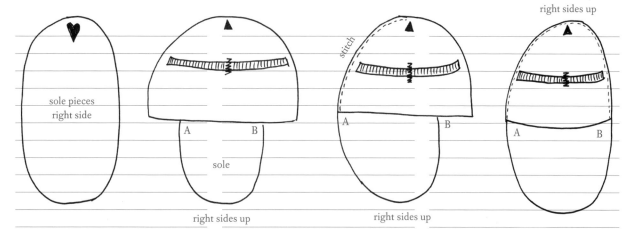

sole pieces right side

A B

sole

right sides up

A B

stitch

right sides up

right sides up

A B

right sides up

9. Attach the sole to the front

◇ Mark the triangle point on the front of shoe piece as shown, with the elastic facing out.
◇ Place the sole piece flat with the heart point at the top.
◇ Place the front of shoe piece on top of the sole piece, matching the heart and triangle points. Pin in the centre to secure.
◇ Stitch the front of shoe to the sole from point A to the triangle point and then to point B. You'll need to work slowly, easing and matching the pieces as you go. Your front of shoe piece is now stitched to the sole. Hurrah!

10. Attach the back to the rest of the shoe

Now attach the back of shoe pieces. Similarly matching and easing, pin the inside (casing) side of the back of shoe piece to the sole, matching the X symbol to the O symbol on each piece. Sew along the unstitched edge of the sole and back of shoe to secure. Sew over this seam again to reinforce.

11. Turn it right side out and thread the elastic

Turn the shoe the right way out. To thread the elastic into the back of shoe, poke a safety pin through one end of the elastic and thread it through the back of shoe casing. Push back the fabric so you have lots of elastic to play with. Keep hold of the other end of the elastic so it doesn't disappear into the casing, and make sure the elastic is not twisted. Pin the two ends of the elastic together then sew firmly together. Now shimmy the fabric along until it hides the elastic altogether.

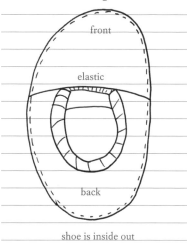

front

elastic

back

shoe is inside out

VOILA!

You made a shoe! Quick, make another cup of tea and then follow the steps again to make the other shoe.

DON'T RUSH and YOU'LL HAVE a lovely pair before you know it!

Fabric clock

It seems so funny that you can make your own clock, doesn't it?
But you really can with this awesome techy project! You could even make a series
of matching panels, with the clock positioned on whichever of them you prefer.

PROJECT BY: LARA CAMERON
SUITABLE FOR: BEGINNERS
SHOULD TAKE: NO MORE THAN 2 HOURS, PLUS DRYING TIME

SHOPPING LIST

◇ A4 piece of chipboard 5 mm thick
◇ 28 cm × 28 cm piece of fabric (you can also use heavy paper)
◇ Can of spray adhesive
◇ Clock numbers and strong craft glue that dries clear and is suitable for gluing the numbers
◇ A clock movement and hands (available at good art or craft stores. The movement should have an 8 mm shaft and the set of hands should have an hour hand that is approximately 80 mm long).
◇ Batteries for the clock movement

CRAFTY NEEDS

◇ Scissors
◇ Rotary cutter and cutting mat are optional but very useful
◇ Compass and pencil
◇ Newspaper or sheets of butcher's paper to cover your work surface so you don't get spray adhesive over it
◇ Ruler
◇ Small paintbrush
◇ Small sharp blade to cut fabric
◇ Strong cutting knife (ask for one where you buy the chipboard)

CUTTING OUT

◇ Measure and cut the chipboard to 210 mm × 210 mm using the cutting knife.

BEFORE YOU START

◇ Make yourself a nice clear space to work in, with a clean work surface.
◇ Be sure you have all your equipment close at hand.
◇ You should work in a well-ventilated space (or wear a mask) when using the spray adhesive. It's pretty pongy.
◇ Cover your work surface with newspaper or butcher's paper.

1. Cut out the centre

Find the centre point of your chipboard – it's 105 mm in from each edge. Using the pencil and compass, draw a circle with a 12 mm diameter in this centre position. Using your cutting knife, carefully cut out the circle you have drawn. This is where the clock movement will fit in.

2. Glue the fabric

It's important to work quickly and confidently when using spray adhesive. Spray one side of the chipboard evenly with the adhesive. On the clean work surface, place your fabric right side down and spray the wrong side of the fabric liberally with spray adhesive. Then take your piece of chipboard (with the hole in the middle) and place it (sticky side down) directly on to the centre of the fabric. There needs to be an even amount of excess fabric on each side.

Make sure there are no bumps and bubbles underneath. Pull the fabric firmly so that it stretches tautly. Pull and fold the edges of the fabric up and around the chipboard and try to make some creases in it (this especially handy if you are using a stiff material that might spring back when you try to glue it).

3. Neaten and fold the corners

Here's the fiddly part – making the corners look nice. Cut and fold the corners as shown in the diagrams at right. You'll need to do this for each corner. You will need to apply a bit

of extra spray adhesive or craft glue here too. Make it nice and neat and smooth. Once you are happy, allow it to dry. Nice work!

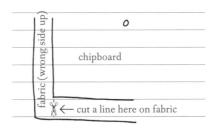

fabric (wrong side up)

chipboard

o

✄ ← cut a line here on fabric

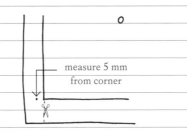

o

measure 5 mm
from corner

✄

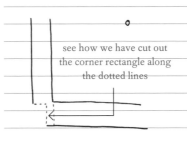

o

see how we have cut out
the corner rectangle along
the dotted lines

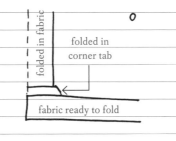

folded in fabric

o

folded in
corner tab

fabric ready to fold

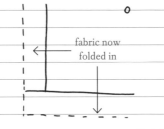

o

fabric now
folded in

4. Attach the numbers

Now that the fabric is neatly covering the chipboard, and the glue is dry, it's time to put the numbers on the front. Glue them on carefully with strong craft glue. Use a small paintbrush to keep things neat. Use all the numbers or just a few – whatever you like. Have some fun and customise it to suit you! That's what craft is all about.

5. Insert the clock movement

Using a sharp blade, carefully cut a 12 mm hole in the fabric, in line with the hole you've already cut in the chipboard.

Insert the movement as per the manufacturer's instructions. Insert the batteries. Set the clock to the correct time, because you're all done. You, crafty person, have made a clock!

You've got no excuses for being late now! If you'd like to make another clock for a friend, you could consider varying the shape or size of the board, and you can vary the placement of the clock movement too – it can be off centre, for instance.

HAVE FUN
making things!

Morris the sensitive panda

Morris is a quiet, sensitive soul. Although he can happily amuse himself,
he does like the company of people, bears and other animals. Wool or wool blends are best for Morris,
but acrylic will work too. Eight-ply yarn is sometimes labelled 'DK' or 'double knitting'.

PROJECT BY: JESS MCCAUGHEY
SUITABLE FOR: CAREFUL, PATIENT BEGINNERS
SHOULD TAKE: SEVERAL HOURS, DEPENDING ON ABILITY

SHOPPING LIST

◇ 40 g of 8-ply knitting yarn in white
◇ 20 g of 8-ply yarn in black
◇ 3 mm crochet hook
◇ Pair of 9 mm safety eyes and metal washers,
  in yellow or the colour of your choice
◇ 15 cm × 15 cm piece of black felt
◇ Black embroidery floss for mouth, nose and eyes
◇ Wool or polyester toy stuffing

CRAFTY NEEDS

◇ Dressmaker's pins
◇ Embroidery or crewel needle
◇ Tapestry needle for sewing up
◇ Stuffing stick, chopstick or pencil to help with stuffing

BEFORE YOU START SEWING

Please see the crochet guide on page 130 if you are new
to crochet.
Take note of the following abbreviations:
dc – double crochet
st(s) – stitch(es)
ch – chain
dec 1 – decrease 1 stitch. To do this, insert hook in next
stitch, yarn round hook, draw through loop twice, draw
through all 3 loops on hook.
inc 1 – increase 1 stitch. To do this, make 2 dc in next stitch.

NOTE

At the end of each round, mark the last stitch with a
contrasting floss or yarn so you can keep track of
where you are.

1. Head (make 1)

Using white, make 2 chain.
Round 1 Miss first chain, 6 dc in next ch (see Note). 6 sts
Round 2 Inc 1 in each st. 12 sts
Round 3 (dc in next st, inc 1) 6 times. 18 sts
Round 4 (dc in next 2 sts, inc 1) 6 times. 24 sts
Round 5 (dc in next 3 sts, inc 1) 6 times. 30 sts
Round 6 (dc in next 4 sts, inc 1) 6 times. 36 sts
Round 7 (dc in next 5 sts, inc 1) 6 times. 42 sts
Round 8 (dc in next 6 sts, inc 1) 6 times. 48 sts
Work 4 rounds straight, without further increase.
Round 13 (dc in next 6 sts, dec 1) 6 times. 42 sts
Round 14 (dc in next 5 sts, dec 1) 6 times. 36 sts
Round 15 (dc in next 4 sts, dec 1) 6 times. 30 sts
Round 16 (dc in next 3 sts, dec 1) 6 times. 24 sts
Round 17 (dc in next 2 sts, dec 1) 6 times. 18 sts
Round 18 (dc in next 4 sts, dec 1) 3 times. 15 sts.
Slip stitch in next st (the stitch at the beginning of
the previous round). Fasten off.

2. Body (make 1)

Using white, make 2 chain.
Round 1 Miss first chain, 6 dc in next ch (see Note). 6 sts
Round 2 Inc 1 in each st. 12 sts
Round 3 (dc in next st, inc 1) 6 times. 18 sts
Round 4 (dc in next 2 sts, inc 1) 6 times. 24 sts
Round 5 (dc in next 3 sts, inc 1) 6 times. 30 sts
Work 4 rounds straight, without further increase
Round 10 (dc in next 3 sts, dec 1) 6 times. 24 sts
Work 4 rounds straight, without further decrease
Round 15 (dc in next 2 sts, dec 1) 6 times. 18 sts
Work 2 rounds straight, without further decrease.
Round 18 (dc in next 4 sts, dec 1) 3 times. 15 sts.
Slip stitch in next st (the stitch at the beginning of
the previous round). Fasten off.

3. Muzzle (make 1)

Using white, make 2 chain.
Round 1 Miss first chain, 6 dc in next ch (see Note). 6 sts
Round 2 Inc 1 in each st. 12 sts
Round 3 1 dc in each stitch. 12 sts.
Slip stitch in next st (the stitch at the beginning of the
previous round). Fasten off.

4. Ears (make 2)

Using black, make 2 chain.
Round 1 Miss first chain, 6 dc in next ch (see Note). 6 sts
Round 2 Inc 1 in each st. 12 sts
Work 2 rounds straight, without further increase.
Slip stitch in next st (the stitch at the beginning of the
previous round). Fasten off.

5. Arms (make 2)

Using black, make 2 chain.
Round 1 Miss first chain, 7 dc in next ch. 7 sts
Round 2 Inc 1 in each st. 14 sts
Work 11 rounds straight, without further increase.
Slip stitch in next st (the stitch at the beginning of the previous round). Fasten off.

6. Legs (make 2)

Using black, make 2 chain.
Round 1 Miss first chain , 6 dc into next ch (see Note). 6 sts
Round 2 Inc 1 in each st. 12 sts
Work 8 rounds straight, without further increase.
Slip stitch in next st (the stitch at the beginning of the previous round). Fasten off.

7. Stuff the head, position the eyes and make the face

Stuff the finished head firmly so there are no gaps or lumps. It should be round and ball-like. Use small pieces of stuffing and the stuffing stick to help you.

Cut the eye patches from black felt. Make a small hole or incision towards the top of each piece of felt so you can insert the eyes. Poke an eye through the incision on each eye patch. Place the eye patches on the head, pushing the back of the eyes through the gaps between stitches. Use the photo at left as a placement guide. Sew the eye patches into position.

EYE TEMPLATE

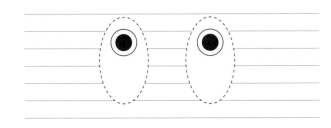

Cut a nose from felt. Pin then sew the nose onto the muzzle, and embroider the mouth using embroidery floss. Pin the finished muzzle to the head. Play around until you are happy and your panda has the personality you want him to have. Don't agonise trying to make him look just like the picture. No two bears are exactly alike. Wonky is good!

When you are happy, remove the pinned muzzle (just for now!) and also remove some of the stuffing so you can access the back bits of the eyes. Securely place washers on the backs of the eye bits that are poking into the head cavity. Restuff the rest of the head, leaving the bottom open. Pin the muzzle on once again and sew to the head using ladder stitch. Fold the ears in half to make semi-circles, pin the ears to the head and sew into place using ladder stitch.

8. Stuff the body and attach the arms and legs

Stuff the body firmly, leaving the neck open. Place the head onto the body and sew together firmly, using small ladder stitches and working along the whole circumference. Make it nice and secure.

Stuff the arms, leaving approximately 1 cm at the top of the arms free of stuffing. Close the openings using a small overcast stitch. Pin the arms on the body, and sew on using ladder stitch.

Stuff the legs firmly, again leaving about 1 cm at the top free of stuffing. Close the openings using overcast stitch, as for the arms.

Turn Morris upside down so his bottom is facing you. Pin the legs on the body, three or four rounds from the centre of his bottom, with the tops of the legs right next to each other. Sew the legs on the body using overcast stitch and a long piece of yarn so that you can secure both legs at the same time. All done! Turn him right side up and there you have him.

LIKE all BEARS Morris LOVES a hug AND a snuggle

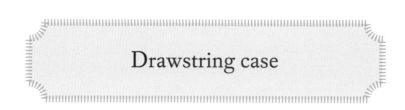

Drawstring case

A crafty way to keep your sunglasses safe. This handmade Zakka-style pouch is super useful.
It looks lovely and helpfully keeps your sunglasses scratch-free and stylish. I think the pen pocket is a
great idea too – especially if your bag is a bit of a vault, like mine is.

PROJECT BY : KRISTEN DORAN
SUITABLE FOR : BEGINNERS
SHOULD TAKE : NO MORE THAN 1 ½ HOURS

SHOPPING LIST

◇ You will need two different fabrics, or three if you want
   to be really tricky. We suggest linen, cotton or denim.
◇ 30 cm × 40 cm piece of Fabric 1
◇ 30 cm × 40 cm piece of Fabric 2
◇ 30 cm × 40 cm piece of Fabric 3 (optional)
◇ 50 cm cord or thin ribbon
◇ 2 beads for decoration (optional)

CRAFTY NEEDS

◇ Sewing machine
◇ Thread to match your fabric
◇ Paper scissors
◇ Fabric scissors
◇ Measuring tape or ruler
◇ Dressmaker's pins
◇ Iron
◇ Seam ripper in case of mistakes
◇ Safety pins

PATTERN NEEDS

There are five pattern pieces. You will need to cut one of
each piece, working out which fabric you would prefer for
the pockets, pen holder and other pieces.

BEFORE YOU START SEWING

◇ Cut out the pieces as detailed above.
◇ Make sure your machine is threaded and your bobbin
   is full.
◇ Note that all seam allowances are 6 mm.
◇ For best results, trim loose threads as you go.
◇ Keep your ruler or measuring tape at hand.
◇ Perhaps make a big cup of tea? Yes, I think so!

1. Make and position the pocket

Fold under 5 mm along the side seams and the bottom seam of the pocket piece and press in place. Fold under 5 mm along the top edge of the pocket and press. Fold under another 5 mm along the top and press again. Stitch across the top to form a hem.

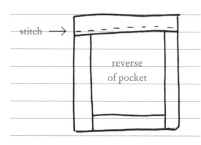

Pin the pocket, right side up, onto the right side of the middle panel of the pouch, as marked on the pattern piece. Stitch into place around sides and bottom as shown, leaving the top of the pocket open.

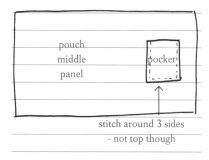

2. Make and position the pen holder

The pen holder is made in similar way to the pocket, except you don't hem the bottom edge. Fold under 5 mm along the two side seams and press. Fold under 5 mm along the top edge of the pen holder pocket and press. Fold the top edge under another 5 mm and press. Stitch across the top hem only.

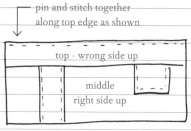

Pin the pen holder pocket, right side up, onto the right side of the middle panel of the pouch as marked on the pattern piece. Stitch along each side (close to the edge – you want your pen to fit!), but leave the top and bottom edges of the pen holder pocket open.

3. Assemble the pouch

With right sides facing and the long edges matched together, pin the top pouch piece to the middle pouch piece. Sew this seam.

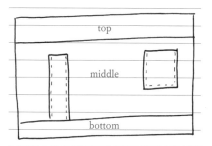

In the same way, pin the bottom pouch piece to the middle pouch piece, with the right sides facing and the long edges matched together. Sew this seam.

Fold it all out and press flat, with the right side facing you. The top, middle and bottom pieces are now all sewn together as one piece.

With right sides together, fold in half crossways (from left to right) as shown in the diagram. Measure 4 cm down from the top right-hand corner and mark close to the edge with a pen. Stitch from this marked point down the side and across the bottom of the pouch.

fold and then stitch around bottom and side leaving a gap as shown

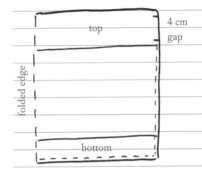

3. Make the base of the pouch flat

With the pouch wrong side out, open out one corner of the bottom of the pouch and then press the corner flat to form a triangle. (Refer to the picture). The seam should be running down the middle of this pressed triangle as shown. Mark a line 3 cm from the point of the triangle. Now sew across this line, as pictured. Trim off the corner 5 mm from the stitching and repeat the whole process for the other corner.

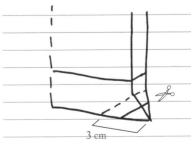

4. Finish the top of the pouch

Remember you left the gap at the top right side? You need to press the raw edge over about 5 mm. Still with the wrong side facing out, pin and then stitch this edge down to meet where you'd previously stitched to, then across the bottom of this point and up to the top edge as shown.

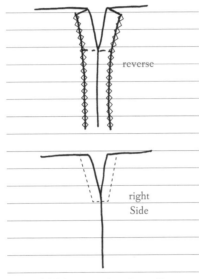

Next, fold the top edge down 5 mm. Press. Then fold it down another 1.5 cm and press again. Stitch carefully around the top of the pouch, creating a casing for you to thread the cord or ribbon through. Nice work!

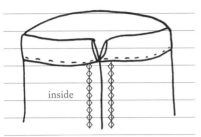

To thread the drawstring, attach a safety pin to the end of the cord or ribbon and use the pin to push through the casing you have just made. Thread all the way through the casing until it comes out the other open end. Now carefully pull (without losing the end!) until the length of the ribbon is even on each side. Tie both ends of the ribbon into a knot, leaving a little extra ribbon to thread your beads onto. Thread the beads. Tie another secure knot and trim any messy ribbon ends.

There you go!
All done!

CHOOSE YOUR cutest BuTtoN & stRing

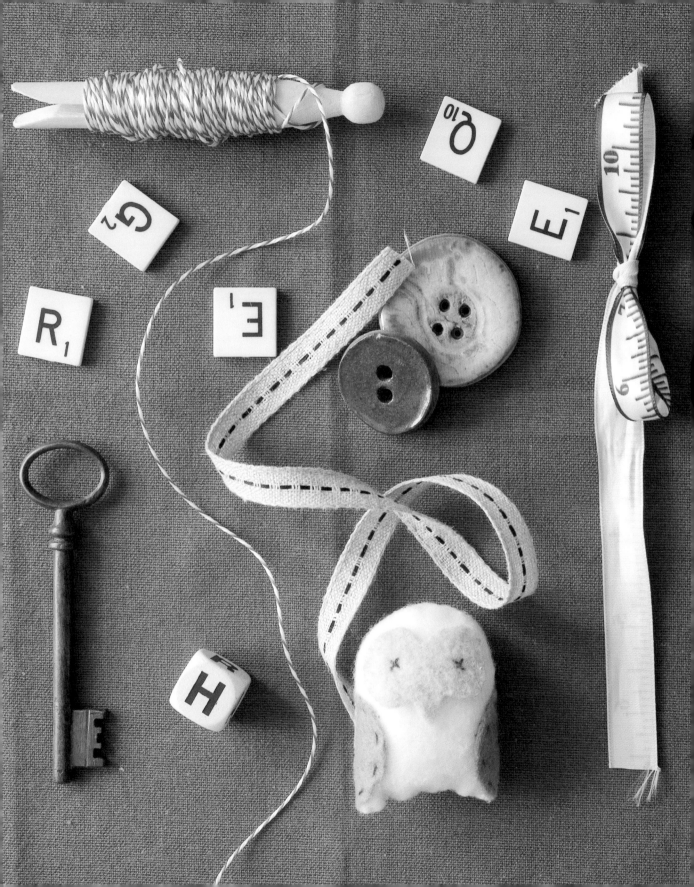

Mini quilt

This tiny quilt is perfect for a doll's bed, but it's also beautiful enough to frame and hang in your favourite room. The simple Japanese 'sashiko' embroidery and pretty, mixed-up cotton panel personalise this project. The lovely linen has an open weave, which makes it just right for stitching projects, and the neutral shade complements the colourful embroidery floss beautifully.

PROJECT BY: ALISON BROOKBANKS
SUITABLE FOR: BEGINNERS
SHOULD TAKE: ABOUT 3 HOURS, INCLUDING THE EMBROIDERY
FINISHED SIZE: 34 CM X 56 CM

SHOPPING LIST

◇ For piece A: 50 cm × 80 cm piece of natural linen (prewashed)
◇ For piece B: 50 cm × 50 cm piece of cotton
◇ For piece C: Three small scraps of assorted cottons. Each scrap should be at least 10 cm wide, and you'll need a total combined length of 50 cm
◇ 80 cm × 50 cm of cotton batting (quilt inlay)
◇ Coloured embroidery floss to match your fabrics

CRAFTY NEEDS

◇ Sewing machine
◇ Thread to match your fabrics
◇ Fabric scissors, or rotary cutter and cutting mat
◇ Measuring tape or ruler
◇ Dressmaker's pins
◇ Iron
◇ Seam ripper in case of mistakes
◇ Air-fading fabric marker or tailor's chalk
◇ Embroidery needle
◇ Safety pins for holding the batting in place

PATTERN NEEDS

◇ For piece A, cut one piece 46 cm × 78 cm.
◇ For piece B, cut two pieces 18 cm × 46 cm.
◇ For piece C, cut your combination of small cotton pieces into 10 cm lengths, then cut these into strips of varying widths of 3 cm, 4 cm and 7.5 cm.
◇ The quilt batting will be cut to size later.

BEFORE YOU START SEWING

◇ Make sure your machine is threaded and your bobbin is full.
◇ Note that seam allowances are 1.5 cm for edge seams and 5 mm for the patchworked cotton fabric strip.
◇ For best results, trim loose threads as you go.
◇ Keep a ruler or tape measure close by for this project.

2. Join the pieces together

Pin the patchworked piece C to a long edge of one of the cotton piece B lengths, right sides facing, and stitch together. Press the seam open.

Now pin the second piece B length to one end (the short edge) of the linen (piece A), right sides facing, and stitch together. Press the seam open.

Pin piece C to the other end (the other short edge) of the linen (piece A), right sides facing. Stitch together, then press the seam open.

Note that the bottom edge of the quilt is folded, rather than sewn. With right sides facing, fold the four-panel fabric piece that you have just created in half widthways. Line up the piece B seams at each side of the quilt, pin in place, and iron the entire body flat, making sure the quilt is sitting square. Sew the side seams.

The top edge (the two cotton piece B pieces) will still be open. Press flat and snip the corners diagonally to ensure a tight corner when the quilt is turned right side out. Turn it right side out, then steam press each seam to lie flat and neat, paying particular attention to the corners.

1. Make the colourful strip first

To make piece C, mix and match the small cotton strips of varying widths to create one long piece. Play around with the combinations, mixing prints and widths, until you're happy with the arrangement. Pin these small pieces together lengthways with right sides facing.

Stitch the pieces together with a 5 mm seam. Press the seams open afterwards. You should now have a long strip of lots of different widths. Perfect. Next, with a rotary cutter or scissors, trim this piece to an even width of 10 cm, and to a length of 46 cm to match the linen and feature panel pieces.

Fabric credits: Amy Butler, Liberty, Honeycomb Kei

3. Embroider the quilt

On the front of the quilt, on the linen panel, draw the circle embroidery design, using tailor's chalk or an air-fading marker and assorted circular objects to trace around. Refer to the photo for placement. An odd number of circles will appear more balanced visually.

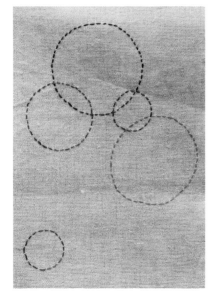

Next, separate your embroidery floss into three strands or threads. Using these three strands of floss, embroider around the circle outlines using sashiko stitch. Sashiko is a form of running stitch with a set repetition of the stitch-to-gap ratio: 3 mm of stitch to 2 mm of gap. Take care to embroider only though one layer of the linen; keep one hand tucked inside the quilt to keep the layers separate.

4. Insert the batting

Measure the quilt top. Cut out a piece of batting to the same size minus 1 cm on one short end (this is to compensate for the seam allowance when you close the remaining seam at the top of the quilt).

When it's cut to the correct size, insert it into the quilt through the top seam, which is still open. Be sure it lies nice and flat and does not buckle or fold. Secure in place with safety pins, pinning from the bottom corners to the open top edge, smoothing as you go.

Next, mark out a line on the linen panel on the front of the quilt, using tailor's chalk and marking about 1 cm outside the seam of the patchwork strip (piece C). This line is for the French knots. Using three strands of floss, embroider French knots along this line, making knots every 1.5 cm. Take the needle directly through *all* layers of the quilt, to the immediate underside, and make another French knot in this exact spot. This way you'll get an even row of French knots on the back of the quilt as well. Neat, huh?

5. Finish the top end of the quilt

Turn each top edge under by about 1 cm, and press in place with a hot iron to form the top hem. Pin in place. Using thread in a matching colour, sew up the top opening using tiny, almost invisible stitches. Iron the seam flat, remove all the safety pins and you're done!

A great way to use old treasured fabrics.

Softie wheat-bag friend

Claire's wheat-bags are not just cute, they are really useful and can make you feel better in so many ways. Wheat-bags are not suitable for small children, but you could make this as a toy for a child or baby by filling it with toy stuffing rather than wheat.

PROJECT BY: CLAIRE ROBERTSON
SUITABLE FOR: BEGINNERS
SHOULD TAKE: NO MORE THAN 1½ HOURS

SHOPPING LIST

◇ 30 cm × 32 cm piece of canvas-weight fabric, such as canvas, corduroy or denim (Fabric 1)
◇ 21 cm × 32 cm piece of contrasting canvas-weight fabric (Fabric 2)
◇ 10 cm × 20 cm piece of gingham or dotted fabric for ear lining
◇ 5 cm × 5 cm scrap of white craft felt
◇ 5 cm × 5 cm scrap of dark-coloured craft felt
◇ Embroidery floss in white, black, red and pink, or colours to match your fabrics
◇ Approximately 800 g of wheat kernels or toy stuffing

CRAFTY NEEDS

◇ Sewing machine
◇ Thread to match your fabric
◇ Paper scissors
◇ Fabric scissors
◇ Measuring tape or ruler
◇ Dressmaker's pins
◇ Iron
◇ Seam ripper in case of mistakes
◇ Embroidery needle
◇ Funnel or A4 piece of paper
◇ Sewing needle

PATTERN NEEDS

There are seven pattern pieces:
◇ Piece A (top panel)
◇ Piece B (face panel)
◇ Piece C (bottom panel)
◇ Piece D (ear)
◇ Piece E (legs and arms)
◇ Piece F (inside eye)
◇ Piece G (outside eye)

YOU WILL NEED TO CUT THE FOLLOWING:

◇ From Fabric 1, cut two of piece A, two of piece C, two of piece D and four of piece E.
◇ From Fabric 2, cut two of piece B and four of piece E.
◇ From the gingham or dot fabric, cut two of piece D.
◇ From the white felt, cut two of piece F.
◇ From the dark felt, cut two of piece G.

BEFORE YOU START SEWING

◇ Make sure your machine is threaded and your bobbin is full.
◇ Note that seam allowances are 1 cm unless it says otherwise.
◇ Sew each seam twice to stop fraying and add strength.
◇ For best results, trim loose threads as you go.
◇ Trim the seams and clip along the curves to give them a nicer shape once they are turned right side out and stuffed.

1. Make the body

With right sides together, pin a piece A to a piece B along the longest edge. Sew the seam. With right sides together again, pin the bottom of piece B to piece C along the longest edge and sew the seam. Repeat with the remaining piece A, piece B and piece C. One of these panels will form the back and the other the front of your softie wheat bag.

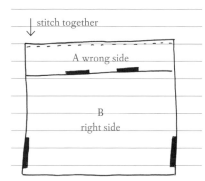

stitch together

A wrong side

B
right side

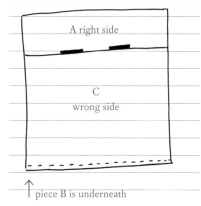

A right side

C
wrong side

piece B is underneath

2. Make the face

Stitch the white felt eye pieces (G) onto the front piccc B to make the face. You can use a backstitch or running stitch to stitch around the edges. Be sure to use only two strands of white embroidery thread for sharp results.

Now, you need to stitch the little dark eye pieces (F) on top of the white felt eyes – refer to the photo as a guide. Add eyelashes using three nice, straight stitches. Stitch a little nose using pink embroidery floss – a small backstitch is fine, or a French knot works a treat. Stitch a mouth with pink embroidery floss, and perhaps some eyebrows if you feel like it.

3. Make the ears

Next, with right sides together, pin the inner ear fabric piece D (the gingham or dot fabric) to the outer ear fabric piece D. Machine sew the curved edges, leaving the straight edge open for turning out. Trim the seams close to the stitching. Clip along the curves to give them a nicer shape if stuffed, and turn right side out. Repeat for the other ear.

On the inside of the ear, where marked on the pattern, pull the gingham or dotted fabric into a pleat and stitch about 3 mm from the edge to hold the pleat in place. Repeat for the other ear.

4. Make the legs and arms

With right sides together, pin the matching limb pieces E together. Machine sew the seam, leaving the short, straight edge open for turning out. Repeat with the other E pieces to give you four lovely limbs in total. Trim the seams close to the stitching and clip along the curves. Turn out the right way.

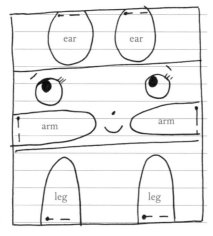

5. Sew it all together

Pin the ears, legs and arms onto the front panel – refer to the diagram. Note that all the limbs should be facing inwards at this stage, so that they don't get caught in the seams. Machine sew into position about 2 mm from the edge to secure.

With this front body panel facing you – and double checking that all the limbs and ears are tucked well inside, away from the seams – place the back body panel (made up of the three smaller panels) over the top, right side facing down, and match the two panels up around all four edges. Pin in place and machine sew all around, leaving a small gap between the legs for turning and filling. Snip the corners, clip the seams close to the stitching and turn out.

6. Fill with wheat

You can use a funnel, or you can make a cone shape from a piece of A4 paper and some sticky tape. Use this to funnel the wheat into the softie bag. Fill with wheat, then tip upside down so you can stitch the opening closed using small, tight stitches.

If stuffing with toy stuffing, stuff slowly and carefully, using small pieces of stuffing, until the shape is firm but cuddly. Then stitch closed with small, tight hand stitches.

Heat the wheat bag for 30 seconds in the microwave on medium–high heat or until it's just warm, not hot (be sure to test the temperature carefully before you use it).

Enjoy!

Safety notes

◇ Do not overheat wheat bags – check the temperature diligently.
◇ Wheat bags should not be given to small children.
◇ Use wheat bags only as a heat pack for direct application to the body. Never use them as bed warmers, as this is a fire risk.
◇ Do not reheat until the wheat bag has completely cooled.
◇ Unpick and refill the bag if the wheat starts to smell toasty.
◇ Do not put wheat bags into storage until they are completely cold.

Phoney flowers

What do you get if you cross a coat hanger with a telephone directory? You get this ace project, designed by eco-crafter Erin Lewis. Make your own paper bouquet, and have a play around with the materials you use. Erin wants you to. If you don't buy anything new, she'll be super pleased.

PROJECT BY: ERIN LEWIS
SUITABLE FOR: BEGINNERS
SHOULD TAKE: ABOUT 30 MINUTES

SHOPPING LIST

◇ Tracing paper (or you could use baking paper)
◇ Stiff cardboard
◇ Yellow Pages or other phone directory – you could also use waxed paper, baking paper, storybook pages, kraft paper, wrapping paper … the list is endless!
◇ Bobby pins for the stamens (or you could use short lengths of string, cotton buds, twist ties, or pieces of fine wire each with a single small bead on the end)
◇ Metal coat hanger for the stem (or you could use jewellery wire – 20-gauge works well – or pre-cut wire florist stems, orphaned or broken knitting needles, or any old wire you find lying around)
◇ Green floristry tape or electrical tape (optional)

CRAFTY NEEDS

◇ Pliers
◇ Scissors
◇ Sticky tape
◇ Wire cutters (or pliers with cutting ability)

PATTERN NEEDS

◇ Cut one from the template overleaf to make one flower.

BEFORE YOU START

◇ Trace the outline of the petal template onto the tracing paper. Tape this to a piece of stiff cardboard and cut around it to create the template.

1. Cut out the petal piece

Position the template onto one page of the phone directory. Trace and cut out a petal sheet from this template. You can cut it with all the petals the same length, or with four shorter petals. This will make one flower.

2. Make the stamen

Connect three or four bobby pins by inserting the leg of one pin through the base of another pin. They'll splay out a bit – try to keep them as close together as possible. Secure them loosely with a piece of sticky tape to avoid too much juggling.

3. Make the petals of the flower

Roll the petal sheet around the stamen like a tube, lining up the bottom of the sheet with the base of the bobby pins. How tightly you roll will determine where your petals fall. Experiment until you find what works best.

Holding the base of the flower together with one hand, carefully peel each petal outward with the other hand, starting from the outermost petal. Coax, ease, bend and shape the petals with your fingers to get the look you want, taking care not to tear them. Wrap a piece of sticky tape around the base of the flower to secure it.

4. Make the stem

Using wire cutters or a sharp set of pliers, cut a 20-cm length of wire. Coat hangers can be tough to cut and bend, so you might need to enlist the help of someone strong, or use one of the alternative wires suggested in the shopping list. Bending the wire is easier without the flower attached. Make two small loops with the wire, then insert the base of the flower into them and squeeze tightly with the pliers to secure.

5. To finish or not to finish?

You can leave your flower unfinished, or use floristry tape or green electrical tape to cover the rest of the stem.

PLACE in a jar or BOTTLE and aDMiRE your HANDIWORK!

Flower template

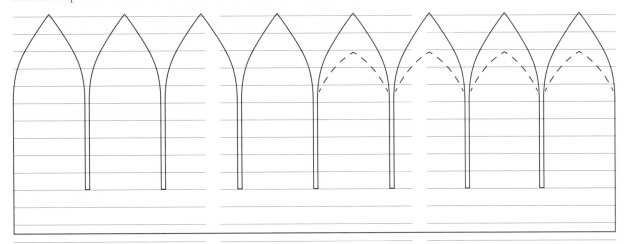

eak.cup of tea.**resume**.

two. .purl one.**333**

eak.**cup of tea**.resume.**reco**

knit one.purl two.

eak.cup of tea.**resume**.reco

.333333. brea

cup of tea.resume.

t.knit one.purl two

cup of tea.**resume**.red

two. .purl one.break.

eak.**cup of tea**.resume.reco

.knit one. knit t

eak.cup of tea.**resume**.reco

two.purl one. br

wake up on the grass...

Berlei
True-to-Type Foundations

HIPS
WAIST WEIGHT
NAME
ADDRESS

Umbrella Prints
umbrellaprints.typ

Moopy's lovely notebook cover

This is the happiest notebook you will ever see.
Could you really be grey with Moopy bunny smiling at you each time you want to write stuff down?

PROJECT BY : CARLY SCHWERDT
SUITABLE FOR : BEGINNERS
SHOULD TAKE : ABOUT 3 HOURS (EMBROIDERY TAKES TIME)

SHOPPING LIST

◇ 30 cm × 60 cm piece of light-coloured linen or open-weave fabric
◇ At least three scraps of complimentary printed cotton fabrics, each 20 cm × 20 cm
◇ Embroidery floss in cream, brown, dark pink, light pink and orange, or colours to match your fabrics
◇ 30 cm of natural-coloured twill (cotton) tape
◇ Small scraps of brown, cream and blue felt
◇ Embroidery hoop
◇ Tracing paper (or you can use baking paper)
◇ A5 notebook

CRAFTY NEEDS

◇ Sewing machine
◇ Thread to match your fabric
◇ Paper scissors
◇ Fabric scissors
◇ Measuring tape or ruler
◇ Dressmaker's pins
◇ Iron
◇ Seam ripper in case of mistakes
◇ Air-fading fabric marker or tailor's chalk
◇ Chopstick or knitting needle, for turning out
◇ Embroidery transfer pencil (this allows you to drawing designs onto paper, which you can then iron onto fabric)
◇ Needle

PATTERN NEEDS

◇ There is one pattern piece, which you will need to cut out twice: once from the linen fabric (for the inside book cover) and once from patched-together scrappy pieces (for the outside book cover). See 'Before you start sewing' for how to make this patchwork piece.

BEFORE YOU START SEWING

◇ Make sure your machine is threaded and your bobbin is full.
◇ Note that seam allowances are 5 mm unless it says otherwise.
◇ Trim loose threads as you go for best results.
◇ To make the patchwork piece, machine sew the cotton scraps together – in any arrangement that you like – to make a rectangular piece 25 cm × 52 cm. It could have three simple panels, or you could patch it together in a more complex way if you know how. Then cut out one pattern piece from this patched fabric piece.
◇ Using a ballpoint pen, trace the embroidery design onto tracing paper or baking paper. Now flip it over and trace on the *other side* with the transfer pencil. This will ensure the design is as shown in our picture, rather than facing the wrong way!
◇ Perhaps a bowl of marshmallows or a hot chocolate might be helpful at this point?

1. Get ready to embroider

Place the Moopy design you have just traced onto the top right-hand corner of the linen fabric piece, positioning it as shown in the diagram. Be sure that the transfer-pencil side is facing down, so that Moopy will transfer correctly. Use two or three pins to pin the paper into place, then iron the transfer onto the fabric. Don't move the iron back and forth, as this will cause the design to smudge. Instead, press down in one place for a few seconds, then lift the iron, move it to another section of the design, and repeat.

How long it takes for the design to transfer will vary according to the iron and brand of transfer pencil you have used – it's not an exact science. Remove one pin and check if your design has transferred. If it's still faint, press some more then check again. Don't completely unpin it until it has transferred nicely.

Remove the paper and check the transfer. If there are bits you can't quite see, just fill them in freehand with an air-fading fabric marker.

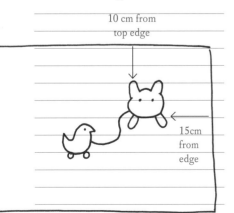

10 cm from top edge

15cm from edge

2. Cut the felt pieces and start stitching

Next, trace over the face shape, both paws and the duck wheels with tracing or baking paper. Pin these traced paper pieces to the coloured felt scraps. Pin the face to the cream felt, the paws to the brown felt and the duck wheels to the blue felt. Cut these shapes out.

Using cream embroidery floss, stitch the face onto the correct spot in the Moopy outline – refer to the photo for placement. You can use whatever stitch you like – blanket stitch, running stitch or just some nice, neat little vertical stitches running around the face.

Use the pink floss to stitch around the outline of Moopy's head, using your preferred stitch – backstitch or running stitch are easy.

Now embroider the face features, using brown floss for the eyes and nose, and pink for the cheeks. Isn't this fun? Continue in the same way, stitching on the felt paws and the duck wheels, outlining the duck, and stitching on the beak, eye and string lead. Keep referring to the photo as a guide.

3. Attach the twill tape

With the right side facing up, pin the twill tape to *each* point A on the *inside* book cover piece (the one without the embroidery) making sure it's nice and straight and even. Stitch into place close to the edge of the book cover piece, about 3 mm in.

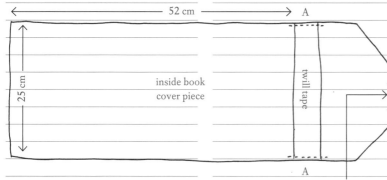

← 52 cm → A

25 cm

inside book
cover piece

twill tape

A

leave open
for turning

4. Sew the book cover together

Now pin the two book cover pieces together, right sides facing each other, with the twill tape hiding in between them. Remembering to leave a 5 cm gap in the short end so you can turn the cover right way out, machine sew these two pieces together about 5 mm in from the edge.

Now, turn the book cover the right way out, push out the corners with a chopstick or knitting needle and iron completely flat. Tuck the raw, unsewn edge inside and out of sight and press neatly. Next, stitch up this hole using tiny invisible stitches such as ladder stitch. Press again and slip your notebook inside.

yippee
YOU'RE DONE!

Hand-printed friendship hankies

This fun inky project is a bit of a stencil-and-screen-printing crash course.
All you need for a crafternoon of messy delight is a good friend to help you and a large flat surface
to work from. You can buy the hankies, or if you're very industrious you can make your own.
You'll need 25 to 30 of them. I know you think you don't want to make that many,
but there's not much point going to all this trouble to print only a few, so go for it!

PROJECT BY: GEMMA JONES
SUITABLE FOR: BEGINNERS
SHOULD TAKE: 3 OR 4 HOURS, INCLUDING DRYING TIME
FINISHED SIZE: 34 CM × 56 CM

SHOPPING LIST

◇ Stencil paper (this is an almost plasticised paper from art
   supply stores – it resists the ink and does not curl)
◇ 1 roll of baking paper
◇ Regular paper
◇ Thick cardboard
◇ Silkscreen (you can buy these ready made from art
   supply stores for as little as $50)
◇ Squeegee (a rubber wedge attached to a long wooden
   handle, used to pull the paint)
◇ Screen-printing ink (make sure you buy ink that's suitable
   for fabric or else it will wash out! Permaset is excellent)
◇ Masking tape (any width will do)
◇ 25 or 30 plain hankies (100% cotton is best)

CRAFTY NEEDS

◇ Paper scissors
◇ Iron
◇ Makeshift clothesline or an indoor drying rack for
   drying the hankies; or use waxed paper
◇ Newspaper for protection (lots!)
◇ Rags to help you keep clean as you work
◇ Very sharp blade (such as a craft knife)
◇ Rubber spatula (a kitchen-type one is dandy)

PATTERN NEEDS

You will need to trace the paper doll shape on page 50
onto tracing paper. Then tape it to some thick cardboard
and cut around the traced outline. Voila, template! Be sure
the cardboard is thick enough to trace around the edge of it.

BEFORE YOU START PRINTING

Printing with a silkscreen involves dragging and pushing
printer's ink through a screen over a stencil. This means
that you cut your stencil – and where you cut a 'space' is
where the ink will appear on your underlying base (be it
paper or fabric). Silkscreening gives a sharp, bold result
and is great for a design that you wish to do in multiples.
You're going to love this!

You can buy screen-printing starter kits that contain a
screen, a squeegee and a bunch of inks for about $100,
and you can use them over and over again. Your local art
supply store or online craft communities such as Craftster
can help with further tips and tricks.

1. Prepare the hankies

Wash the hankies and iron them flat. Arrange them in a pile, paying attention to whether there is a back and front. They all need to be ready to print and the right way up.

2. Making the stencil

We're harking back to kindergarten days and using a paper doll chain as our stencil. To make the chain, take a strip of regular paper as wide as your screen and 5–6 cm high. Fold it in a zig-zag back-and-forth way (not over and over) into even accordion pleats the width of the doll template. Trace the doll shape from the cardboard template you made earlier onto the front, making sure the hands touch the edge. This is very important, as it will ensure that the dolls are holding hands in a chain.

With scissors, carefully cut your dolls out, then unfold them. Hopefully they are holding hands – if not, it's back to the drawing board for you, crafter!

Place this doll-chain template onto the tracing paper and trace around the edge of it. You should be able to get at least two rows of dolls, maybe even three, onto the stencil paper. Refer back to your hanky, checking its size to see how many rows you might fit on it. Use a sharp blade to cut around the lines of the dolls. (We didn't fold the stencil paper itself because it's best to keep it nice and flat.) If you want to get fancy, you can carefully cut designs – such as simple love hearts, flowers, diamonds, letters or dots – with your blade into the dresses of your dolls.

You should now have two or three neat chains of dolls on your stencil paper ready to use on your hanky project.

3. Preparing the screen

If you are new to silkscreening, you should do a quick get-to-know-you. The flat underside of the screen that presses up against your hankies is called the print-side, and the front of the screen, which sits recessed within the wooden frame, is called the squeegee-side.

Make sure the screen is clean. Any blockages or dirt will affect the print quality. Attach your rows of paper dolls to the print-side of the screen with masking tape. Adjust them so that their height fits in relation to the size of the hankies. We've allowed them to run wider than the hankies to help with easy registration. This means you don't have to get things lined up too carefully.

Hold the screen up and admire it – all the cut-out or exposed parts will be the parts that get printed. You could add some fancy strips at the top and bottom with little cut-outs if you like. It's up to you!

A cup of tea with extra sugar might be in order now – you'll need extra fortitude for the next part of the project.

4. Get printing

You and your lovely assistant are about to become a mini production line – you must work confidently and swiftly so that the screen doesn't dry up. If that happens, it will be impossible to keep printing – so quick sticks! You can definitely make 25 or 30 hankies without getting exhausted!

Set yourselves up with:
◇ A completely clear tabletop area
◇ A pile of unfolded newspaper on which you are going to print. This protects the tabletop and also provides a semi-cushiony surface to print on
◇ A pile of baking paper cut or torn into roughly hanky-sized pieces
◇ Your jar of ink and spatula at the ready
◇ The pile of neatly ironed hankies
◇ The prepared screen and squeegee

Let's go! Place a piece of baking paper on the pile of newspaper to protect the hanky. Place your first hanky right side up on top of the baking paper. It should be in the middle of the table, with you on one side armed with ink and squeegee and your friend on the other side of the table ready to assist.

Lower your screen onto the hanky, lining the design up as best you can. Registration isn't too vital for this project as the design is forgiving, but you still want to visually line things up as you go.

Get your friend to firmly hold the screen down so it resists movement. With your spatula, dollop some ink across the top of the screen, just above the design. Spread it across in a gloopy line with the spatula. With the squeegee at a 45-degree angle to the screen, drag the ink down across the design towards you, using firm, even pressure and thus pushing the ink through the screen. You may wish to turn your squeegee and give it a second go, pushing upwards and away from you too.

Put your squeegee down, resting it on its wooden handle, then with the help of your friend lift the screen to reveal your first work of art – wow! Remove the printed hanky and let it dry, either hanging neatly somewhere or resting on a piece of waxed paper. Remove the inky sheets of baking paper and newspaper that were under your hanky, revealing a fresh sheet of newspaper, and repeat. Use the spatula to scrape the ink off the squeegee as you go.

CUTE
hanky!

Permaset inks can be cleaned with water and are non-toxic. Make sure you wash the screen really, really, really thoroughly when you're all done. Any left-behind paint that dries on the screen will make it harder to make nice, clean prints in the future.

Heat setting

Let the hankies dry for a couple of hours, then press each hanky with a hot iron for about a minute. This will set the ink and make it resistant to washing. Once the hanky has been washed the ink will soften up and be nose friendly!

Cutest ever baby knickers

Create some adorable puffy pants for your favourite weeny one! These are especially cute when made from vintage sheeting – even a perfectly pressed pillowcase would have the right amount of fabric for these sweet pants. You can adjust the waist and leg elastic to suit babies of various sizes.

PROJECT BY: NICHOLA PRESTED
SUITABLE FOR: BEGINNERS
SHOULD TAKE: ABOUT 1 HOUR

SHOPPING LIST

◇ 50 cm of fabric 115 cm wide or a vintage cotton sheet or pillowcase
◇ 45 cm of 1-cm wide elastic for the waist
◇ 44 cm of 5-mm wide elastic for the legs
◇ 2 or 3 medium-sized safety pins for threading elastic
◇ 2 or 3 small safety pins for threading elastic

CRAFTY NEEDS

◇ Sewing machine
◇ Thread to match your fabric
◇ Paper scissors
◇ Fabric scissors
◇ Measuring tape or ruler
◇ Dressmaker's pins
◇ Iron
◇ Seam ripper in case of mistakes
◇ Perhaps a packet of boiled lollies to keep your strength up!

PATTERN NEEDS

◇ There is one pattern piece and you will need to cut it out twice.

BEFORE YOU START SEWING

◇ Cut out the pattern pieces as detailed above.
◇ Make sure your machine is threaded and your bobbin is full.
◇ Note that seam allowances are 1 cm unless it says otherwise.
◇ For best results, trim loose threads as you go.
◇ A favourite DVD playing in the background would be good, as would something nice to sip while you sew.

Cutting Guide for 34 ins. to 38 ins. bust

Bust **34"**　　Waist **28"**　　Hips **38"**

Hip Measurements

Cutting Guide for 34 to 36

9874 B

Teenage Frock, 9874
30, 32, 34 and 36 ins. Bust

Material Required:

HALF FRONT SKIRT.

HALF BACK SKIRT.

SIDE BACK SKIRT

7 ♠

1. Sew the two pieces together

With right sides facing, pin the two pieces together matching seam A and seam B of each piece. Sew along seam A as marked on the pattern (this is the front seam). Now, sew along seam B (this is the back seam). Keeping the pieces wrong side out, press these seams flat.

2. Make the gusset

Open the pants out so the seams run down the centre of the back and front. Next match the gusset (C) pieces and stitch together as shown. Press this seam flat too. See how easy this is?

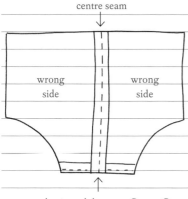

match, pin and then sew Gusset C
front and back together

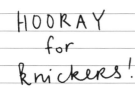

3. Make the waistband

You should still have the wrong sides facing out. Turn down 1 cm along the top edge (the waistband D) and press. Turn down another 1.5 cm and press to create the casing for the elastic. Stitch almost all the way around the top of the pants as shown, being sure to leave a gap for threading the elastic into the fabric channel you've just created.

Stitch right around the waistband as shown – but leave a gap to thread elastic later on!

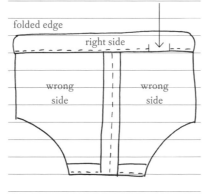

4. Thread the waist elastic

Take the 1 cm wide elastic and poke a safety pin through it, closing the pin carefully. Now poke it into the gap you left in the waistband, and gently push the elastic-pulling pin through the casing. You need to push it through until it has threaded the elastic all the way around the casing (making sure you don't let the other end slip into the casing also). Then push it out the gap again. Easy!

Pull out a few centimetres of excess elastic, overlap them and machine sew back and forth over the two ends a few times until they are secured sturdily together. You don't want this to come undone! Now push the end back into the waistband and stitch up the gap by hand or machine.

5. Elasticise the leg holes

Take the measured leg elastic piece and cut it in half, giving one piece for each leg. The pants should still be wrong side out. Now make the casing in a similar way that you did for the waistband. Fold in the leg edge 5 mm and stitch into place (it's a bit tricky to pin it), then fold in 1 cm more and stitch all around again to create a casing, leaving a little gap open for threading. Thread the elastic and secure the ends as before.

Snip off all loose threads, turn right side out and your project is complete.

Udderly lovely cow

This cow is lovely to look at and not too tricky to make, either. You should know, however, that she's not into running about the pasture, much preferring to doodle in her journal, listen to The Shins and study her French–English dictionary. Make her for someone extra special.

PROJECT BY: FLISS DODD
SUITABLE FOR: THE CONFIDENT BEGINNER
SHOULD TAKE: ABOUT 3 HOURS

SHOPPING LIST

◇ Fliss encourages you to use recycled fabrics, such as old pillowcases and tablecloths.
◇ 40 cm × 40 cm piece of printed fabric
◇ 40 cm × 40 cm piece of plain fabric – denim is good and sturdy
◇ 20 cm × 20 cm piece of tan felt for the horns
◇ 20 cm × 20 cm piece of white felt for the face
◇ 10 cm × 10 cm piece of red felt for the heart
◇ Black embroidery floss
◇ Polyester or wool toy stuffing

CRAFTY NEEDS

◇ Sewing machine
◇ Thread to match your fabric
◇ Paper scissors
◇ Fabric scissors
◇ Dressmaker's pins
◇ Iron
◇ Seam ripper in case of mistakes
◇ Chopstick or pencil for turning out

PATTERN NEEDS

◇ There are eight pattern pieces: body, head, arm, leg, ear, horn, face and heart. Make sure you cut them all out! (You will have 22 individual pieces when you are done.)
◇ Cut one body in printed fabric and one in plain fabric.
◇ Cut one head in printed fabric and one in plain fabric.
◇ Cut two arms in printed fabric and two in plain fabric.
◇ Cut two legs in printed fabric and two in plain fabric.
◇ Cut two ears in printed fabric and two in plain fabric.
◇ Cut four horns from white felt.
◇ Cut one face from white felt.
◇ Cut one heart from red felt.

BEFORE YOU START SEWING

◇ Cut out the pattern pieces as detailed above.
◇ Make sure your machine is threaded and your bobbin is full.
◇ Note that seam allowances are 5 mm unless it says otherwise.
◇ For best results, trim loose threads as you go.
◇ Trim the seams and clip along the curves to give them a nicer shape once they are turned right side out and stuffed.

1. Sew the heart and face

Pin the red felt heart to the printed fabric body piece (the front of the cow). Stitch into place neatly. You can do this by hand or machine, as you prefer – although hand stitching will be cuter!

Pin the white felt face piece to the plain fabric head piece and sew neatly into place. Stitch eyes, nose and mouth onto the lovely oval of the cow's white felt face using the photo as a guide.

2. Make the head and body

The front of the cow

With right sides together, pin the plain fabric head piece to the patterned body piece along seam A. Sew the seam, then stitch over it again for added strength. Open out and iron flat, pressing the seam towards the body piece. To reinforce, topstitch two or three neat lines of stitching on the body piece, just under where the two pieces join. You should be going through all layers of the seam.

The back of the cow

With right sides together, pin the patterned head piece to the plain body piece along seam A. Sew the seam, then stitch over it again for added strength. Open out and iron flat, pressing the seam towards the body piece. Topstitch two or three times along the seam, as previously.

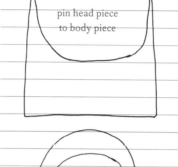

pin head piece to body piece

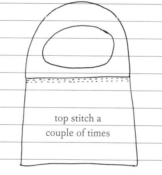

top stitch a couple of times

Make the horns

Take two matching horn pieces and sew together along the curved edge, leaving the short, straight edge open for turning out. Go over the stitching one more time to reinforce. Clip little triangles out of the excess fabric of the seam so that it curves nicely when you turn it out. Turn right side out, using a chopstick or the end of a pencil to turn the horn out right to the tip and make it nice and pointy. Make another horn in the same way.

Make the ears

With right sides facing, sew one plain ear piece to its matching patterned ear piece along the curved edge, leaving the short, straight edge open for turning out. Go over the stitching one more time to reinforce. Clip the curves as previously. Turn right side out in the same way that you did the horns. Press flat. Repeat the whole process with the other two ear pieces.

Make the arms

With right sides facing, sew one plain arm piece to its matching patterned arm piece along the curved edge, leaving the short, straight edge open for turning out. Go over the stitching one more time to reinforce, as before. Clip the curves. Turn right side out and press flat. Now topstitch around the curved edge of the arm piece – this is only for decoration, as the arms will not be stuffed. Repeat to make another arm.

Make the legs

Take one plain leg piece and its matching patterned leg piece. Sew together, stitch again, clip the curves, turn out the right way and press flat, as for the previous steps. Make another leg.

3. Put it all together

Fold the ears in half, with the printed fabric on the inside. With the folded edge at the top, pin one ear to each side of the front of the head at point B. Point the ears inwards, aligning their raw (short) edges with the raw edge of the head piece. Refer to the diagram. (They need to point inwards so that they don't caught in the seam once you sew the cow up.)

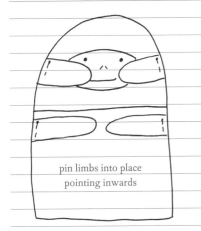

pin limbs into place
pointing inwards

Now pin the arms into place at point C on each side of the front of the body. The arms also need to point inwards, like the ears. Once all the pieces are pinned into place, the face should be facing you (but hiding beneath the ears a bit).

With its right side down, lay the sewn-together back of the cow on top of the front piece. Pin together, matching the seams at the sides. Sew together around the curved edge, leaving the bottom edge open so you can turn it out and stuff it.

4. Turn out and stuff

Turn your cow out the right way and press flat. Stuff the legs and horns firmly with the toy stuffing. Use a chopstick or knitting needle to push the stuffing into the corners if you need to. Next, stuff the body, leaving some room at the bottom to put the legs in and hem it.

5. Finish it off

Turn under the bottom hem by about 5 mm to make a neat edge. Place the legs inside the cow, with the open ends tucked safely inside the body. Pin, then machine sew along the bottom carefully about 5 mm in from the edge of the body. Just go halfway, then stop and check if you need more stuffing. If you do, pop some more in. Then continue to sew along the bottom so that the other leg is sewn into place. Sew along the bottom one more time to reinforce.

6. Attach the horns

Trim the bottom of the horns so they have a neat edge and are both the same length. Hand stitch into place with nice little stitches.

♡ HUG YOUR COW!

Shopping bag keep-safe

A vintage twist on the bag tidy. Even people who use eco-bags as much as possible still end up with rogue plastic bags roaming the wilds of their kitchen. This tidy-made-from-a-tea-towel will keep them stowed and ready for re-use while prettying up your recycling.

PROJECT BY: ANGELA WHITE
SUITABLE FOR: BEGINNERS
SHOULD TAKE: ABOUT 1 HOUR

SHOPPING LIST

◇ One smallish vintage tablecloth or two vintage tea-towels
◇ Matching thread
◇ One packet of snap fasteners with tool included
◇ Hammer

CRAFTY NEEDS

◇ Sewing machine
◇ Thread to match your fabric
◇ Paper scissors
◇ Fabric scissors
◇ Measuring tape or ruler
◇ Dressmaker's pins
◇ Iron
◇ Seam ripper in case of mistakes

PATTERN NEEDS

There are four pattern pieces. Cut one each of the following:
◇ Piece A (strap)
◇ Piece B (front top)
◇ Piece C (front bottom)
◇ Piece D (rear of bag)

BEFORE YOU START SEWING

◇ Cut out the pattern pieces as detailed above.
◇ Make sure your machine is threaded and your bobbin is full.
◇ Note that seam allowances are 1 cm unless it says otherwise.
◇ For best results, trim loose threads as you go.

1. Make the strap

The strap will become the loop from which you hang the bag. With wrong sides together, fold the strap piece A in half lengthways. Iron flat along the fold.

Open the strap out again, and place it wrong side up. Fold both edges into the middle, to meet the ironed-in crease. Now fold the entire shebang in half again lengthways and press. The width of the strap should be about 3 cm. Pin along the open side and sew a seam 3 mm in from the edge. Topstitch another seam 3 mm in from the other edge. Press. Your strap is complete. Make a quick cup of tea and continue.

2. Make the bag

Hem the bottom edge of the front top piece B. To do this, with the wrong side facing you, fold in 1 cm of fabric. Press, then fold in another 1 cm of fabric to form a double hem. Sew along this hem to secure.

Hem the top edge of the front bottom piece C in exactly the same way.

3. Attach the strap

Measure 8 cm in from each side of front top piece B. Keeping the raw edges of the front top piece B level with the ends of the strap, pin the strap into place on the front side to form a V shape. Now stitch 3 mm in from the edge of front top piece B. Refer to the diagram to help you.

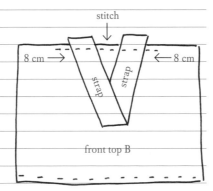

4. Attach the front to the back

With right sides facing, match the unhemmed edge of the front bottom piece C to the bottom of the rear of bag piece D. Pin into place.

With right sides facing, match the unhemmed edge of the front top piece B to the top edge of the rear of bag piece D. The strap will be sandwiched in between these two pieces, still in a downward-pointing V. Pin into place. You're nearly there!

Note that the two hemmed edges should overlap each other in the middle. They need to do this so that you can later attach the snap fastener, and also so the bags can't escape.

Stitch all around the four sides of the bag now. Then zig-zag around for extra strength. Turn right side out, via the hemmed opening, and press.

5. Attach the snap fastener

Match the opening edges neatly, and mark where the snap fastener should go with a couple of pieces of sticky tape. It needs to be right in the centre, with both sides lined up. Be careful not to put it through the back layer of the bag as well – just the two front pieces. Attach using the directions on the snap fastener pack (this is where you need the hammer).

Now stuff it with all those pesky bags that are bumping around your pantry, hang it somewhere convenient and admire your useful handiwork.

Cute-as-a-button vintage clutch

Kara's cute-as-a-button clutch is the perfect popping-out purse.
It'll fit your phone, cash and keys. And the wrist strap makes it helpfully hands free!
It's magically lined – so follow the instructions *carefully* the first time – and once
you've got the hang of it, have fun playing around with other fabrics.

PROJECT BY: **KARA SMITH**
SUITABLE FOR: **CAREFUL, PATIENT BEGINNERS**
SHOULD TAKE: **ABOUT 1 HOUR**

SHOPPING LIST

◇ One vintage tea-towel (or 50 cm × 50 cm piece of
another fabric) for the outside of the purse body
◇ One vintage pillowcase (or 50 cm × 50 cm piece of
another fabric) for the inside of the purse body, the wrist
strap and the purse flap
◇ 50 cm × 50 cm piece of medium-weight iron-on interfacing
◇ Pretty button
◇ Thread – bright colours are good!
◇ Large press stud

CRAFTY NEEDS

◇ Sewing machine
◇ Fabric scissors
◇ Dresmaker's pins
◇ Iron
◇ Seam ripper in case of mistakes
◇ Needle

PATTERN NEEDS

There are three pattern pieces: purse body,
purse flap and wrist strap.
◇ Cut two purse body pieces from the tea-towel.
◇ Cut two purse body pieces from the pillowcase.
◇ Cut two purse flap pieces from the pillowcase.
◇ Cut two purse body pieces from the interfacing.
◇ Cut one purse flap piece from the interfacing.
◇ Cut one wrist strap from the pillowcase.

BEFORE YOU START SEWING

◇ Make sure your machine is threaded and your bobbin
is full.
◇ Note that seam allowances are 1 cm unless it says
otherwise.
◇ For best results, trim loose threads as you go.
◇ Trim and clip inside seams as you go for super-neat
seams on the outside.

1. Mark the fabric pieces

On the right side of the tea-towel purse body pieces, mark the little spot where the strap should be attached as detailed on the purse body pattern – it's fine to just make a tiny cross right on the edge with a pen. Next, mark points C and D on the *wrong* side of the pillowcase purse body pieces.

2. Attach the interfacing

Iron the matching interfacing pieces onto the back of both tea-towel purse body pieces. Be sure to put the shiny side facing down, as this is the side with the adhesive on it. Iron the matching interfacing piece onto one of the pillowcase purse flap pieces. The pieces are now ready to sew!

3. Make the wrist strap

Fold in the edge of the wrist strap piece (as marked on the pattern piece) along the first dotted line. Press. Fold it in again along the next dotted line. Press. Do the same for the other long side of the wrist strap piece. Fold it once more, making sure the long edges meet, creating one long skinny piece. Press again and machine topstitch along one long edge, then along the other long edge for neatness and niceness. Your strap is done!

4. Attach the wrist strap

Fold the wrist strap in half. Pin it to the right side of the tea-towel purse body piece where you marked it earlier. Align the raw end of the strap with the raw edge of the purse body piece, so that the strap is lying across the tea-towel purse piece with the looped end on the left side.

5. Sew the tea-towel purse body pieces together

Lay the other tea-towel body piece on top of the first, with the right side facing in. Sew all around the edge from point A to point B, about 1 cm in from the edge, leaving the long top edge open. Sew along the seam again to reinforce the purse. Trim the edges if it's a bit wonky. Turn it the right way out, remove the pin and press it neatly.

6. Sew the pillowcase purse body pieces together

With right sides facing, pin the two pillowcase purse body pieces together. Sew from point A to point C, then from point B to point D. Don't worry that there is a gap at the bottom – it needs to be there! Again, leave the long top edge open. Trim the edges, but *don't* turn it the right way out. We need it to be inside out.

7. Make the purse flap

With right sides facing, pin the two pillowcase purse flap pieces. Sew from point E to point F, along the curved edge only, and again leaving the long top edge open. Trim the edges and turn it the right way out. Press neatly. Machine topstitch around the curved edge, 5 mm in, as shown in the photo.

8. Sew the lining and the outside together

Lay the tea-towel purse body in front of you, with the strap on the left side. Now, pin as shown through the top three layers of fabric only. The pins should be about 2 cm from the top edge so you don't sew them into the lining. Next, pin the strap as shown. Now gently slide this whole pinned sandwich, strap and all, into the (still inside out) pillowcase purse body piece. Weird, huh?

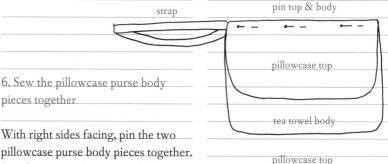

strap

pin top & body

pillowcase top

tea towel body

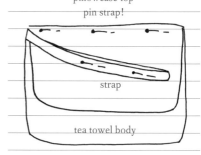

pillowcase top

pin strap!

strap

tea towel body

Next, work out where to sew it up. Pull the pieces apart gently and peer in. When you can see the *wrong* side of your tea-towel pieces, with a seam running down the middle, you've got it right.

Pin the pieces together around the top edge. Be very sure when it's all pinned that you can open it up and see that tea-towel wrong side! Now sew 1 cm in all the way around that top unsewn edge. Take all the pins out. Take a deep breath!

9. Turn it all the right way

Here's the magical part. You left a gap in the bottom of the pillowcase purse body pieces – use that to pull the whole thing back out the right way. Just keep pulling until you've got the tea-towel side right side out!

10. Stitch closed the raw edge

Stitch along the pillowcase body (which is now right side out also) to close it all up neatly. Tuck the pillowcase lining into the tea-towel outer, fold the flap down and press.

11. Attach press stud and button

Hand sew the press stud on the inside flap and body, matching it carefully to allow it to close neatly, then sew the decorative button onto the outside of the flap. It will cleverly cover any messy hand stitching.

HURRAH!
have a bit of a
lie down and
then make one
for a friend.

Butterfly Evelyn

Pretty Evelyn is a perfectly charming soft-toy
companion to help you while away a crafty afternoon.

PROJECT BY: SUZIE FRY
SUITABLE FOR: CONFIDENT BEGINNERS
SHOULD TAKE: ABOUT 2 HOURS

SHOPPING LIST

◇ 20 cm × 25 cm piece of fabric for the body
◇ 20 cm × 25 cm piece of contrast fabric for the wings
◇ 10 cm × 25 cm piece of iron-on medium-weight
   interfacing to stiffen the wings
◇ White felt craft square for eyes and hands
◇ 20 cm of twisted cotton cord for antennae
◇ 50 cm of twisted cord or cotton tape
◇ Appliqué pins
◇ Embroidery floss or contrast thread for stitching eyes,
   nose and mouth
◇ Polyester or wool toy stuffing

CRAFTY NEEDS

◇ Sewing machine
◇ Thread to match your fabric
◇ Paper scissors
◇ Fabric scissors
◇ Measuring tape or ruler
◇ Iron
◇ Seam ripper in case of mistakes
◇ Chopstick or knitting needle for turning out
◇ Needle

PATTERN NEEDS

There are four pattern pieces: body/head, wing, eye and foot.
◇ From the body fabric, cut two body/head pieces.
◇ From the wing fabric, cut four wing pieces.
◇ From the interfacing, cut two wing pieces.
◇ From the felt, cut two eye pieces.
◇ From the felt, cut twelve foot pieces.

BEFORE YOU START SEWING

◇ Make sure your machine is threaded and your bobbin
   is full.
◇ Note that seam allowances are 5 mm unless it says
   otherwise.
◇ Sew each seam twice to add strength.
◇ For best results, trim loose threads as you go.
◇ Keep your stitches small and careful.

1. Make the legs

Cut the cotton tape or cord into six 8-cm pieces. To attach the feet, sew two rectangular foot pieces together, sandwiching one end of the cord or tape in between each to form a foot.

You can stitch the feet to look like claws and trim the original rectangular feet into ovals like in our photo, or you can make the feet and stitching any shape you like. Have fun and use your imagination. It's a good idea to practise on a scrap of felt first.

2. Make the face

On the right side of one body piece, pin the felt eyes into place. Hand sew around the eyes with a running or backstitch to secure. Using a dark colour, make a few satin stitches to form the pupils. Next, stitch a small nose, also in satin stitch, and then a line of backstitch for the mouth. Feel free to vary the suggested stitches if you have your own great ideas.

3. Make the wings

Iron the shiny side of the interfacing wing pieces on to the wrong side of two fabric wing pieces. (The shiny side of the interfacing has the glue on it, so that is the side that has to face the wrong side of the fabric.)

Next, with right sides together, sew one interfaced and one non-interfaced wing piece together around the edge, leaving a small opening along the straight (inner) edge as marked on the pattern for turning out. Turn the wing through to the right side and tuck the seam allowance into the opening. Press the unstitched opening together with a hot iron, tucking any raw edges inside the wing. Using the sewing machine, neatly stitch the opening closed. Do the same with the other two wing pieces.

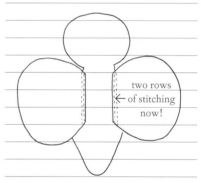

two rows
← of stitching
now!

Pin the finished wings to the right side of the back body piece. Refer to the pattern for suggested placement. Carefully and neatly machine sew the wings to the back body piece, using two rows of stitching as shown in the diagram.

Fold the wings back on themselves to make sure they do not get caught in the seams when you later sew the back body to the front. Use pins to keep them in place.

4. The legs and antennae

With the right side of the front body piece facing up, pin the legs and antennae in place, (referring to the pattern for placement). Make sure the feet and antennae knots are facing into the body (*not* hanging over the edges). It should look like the picture below.

Note: Limbs and antennae must point in. Stitch them into place close to the edge.

Sew in place about 3 mm from the cut edge of the body fabric. You do not want this stitching to show after the body is assembled, but it will eliminate the need for awkward pins while sewing small pieces together.

5. Sew together

Place the back body piece over the front body piece, right sides down. The two body pieces should have their right sides facing each other, with the legs, antennae and wings sandwiched between them. Before you sew, double-check that all these pieces are facing away from the edges and are tucked into the butterfly body. Use lots of pins to keep everything in place.

Stitch all around the body, leaving an opening for turning and stuffing as marked on the pattern. Stitch again for extra strength.

6. To Finish

Using the opening at the side of the body, gently turn the body right side out. Be careful with those butterfly wings. As you turn, all the legs, wings and antennae will pop out. Using a chopstick or knitting needle, carefully push the seams right out.

Start stuffing the body with small pieces of stuffing, concentrating first on the head and then the bottom tip of the body. Stuffing firmly will help to ensure the finished toy is not lumpy. Using ladder stitch or similar, and tiny stitches, sew the opening closed. Then say, 'Pleased to meet you, Evelyn!'

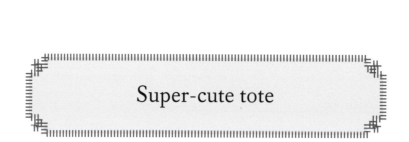

Super-cute tote

A lovely bag for crafty girls. Make this bag and carry it cheerily through a daisy-filled park while humming 'Sunny Side of the Street'. I promise it will make you super-happy. It would be extra good if it were filled with candy-striped sweets, French perfume and lace handkerchiefs.

PROJECT BY: JENNIE MCCLELLAND
SUITABLE FOR: BEGINNERS
SHOULD TAKE: ABOUT 1 ½ HOURS

SHOPPING LIST

◇ One fat quarter (a piece about 46 cm × 56 cm; see Note) of printed cotton for the outside and handle of the bag (Fabric 1)
◇ 50 cm × 90 cm piece of printed cotton for the bag top and bag lining (Fabric 2). Both fabrics should be of similar weight.

CRAFTY NEEDS

◇ Sewing machine and thread
◇ Paper scissors
◇ Fabric scissors
◇ Measuring tape or ruler
◇ Dressmaker's pins
◇ Iron
◇ Seam ripper in case of mistakes
◇ Needle
◇ Tailor's chalk

PATTERN NEEDS

There are four pattern pieces: bag body, handle, bag top and bag lining.
◇ From Fabric 1, cut two bag body pieces.
◇ From Fabric 1, cut two handle pieces.
◇ From Fabric 2, cut two bag top pieces.
◇ From Fabric 2, cut two bag lining pieces on the fold as marked.

BEFORE YOU START SEWING

◇ Cut out the pattern pieces as detailed above.
◇ Make sure your machine is threaded and your bobbin is full.
◇ For best results, trim loose threads as you go.
◇ Mark the triangular pleats on the wrong side of the bag body fabric (but not the lining) with the tailor's chalk.
◇ Put on some 'sunny day' music to get you in the mood.

NOTE

A 'fat quarter' is a standard pre-cut size of fabric used for patchwork and other crafts. You'll find a dizzying array to choose from at your local patchwork shop or online.

So Elizabeth owned up. 'I did it,' she said.

'Well, Elizabeth, perhaps you would like to know that I don't allow behaviour like that in *my* class,' said Miss Ranger. 'Don't do it again.'

'I shall if I want to,' said Elizabeth. Everybody looked at her in amazement. Miss Ranger was surprised.

'You must be very bored with these lessons to want to flip paper about,' she said. 'Go outside the room and stay there till you feel it would bore you less to come back than to stand outside. I don't mind how long you stand there, but I do mind anybody being bored in my class. Now, children, get out your paint-boxes, please.'

There was a clatter as the desks were opened and paint-boxes were taken out. Elizabeth loved painting and was very good at it. She wanted to stay. She sat on in her desk and didn't move.

'Elizabeth! Go outside, please,' said Miss Ranger. There was no help for it then – up Elizabeth got and went outside the door.

'You may come back when you think you can really behave yourself, and not disturb my class,' said Miss Ranger.

It was very dull standing outside the door. Elizabeth wondered if she should wander away and have a swing. No – she might meet the Beauty and the Beast! Ha ha! She was being naughty all right!

But it *was* dull standing so long outside a door and hearing happy talking coming from inside, as the children painted blue and pink lupins that Miss Ranger had brought in. Elizabeth couldn't bear it any longer. She

d, in a low voice to
ithout a smile.
's no time for you to
re sums!'
angrily. 'Well – I'll
t of something really

she w
asked to do s

All the chi
two mistresses a
Elizabeth! How
felt Ruth's hard
move! She glar
speak angrily to her w
mer being rapped
'Sit, please,' said one the everyone sat. Eliza-beth saw that there was a wooden hammer or mallet on the table in front of the judge, and also a large notebook

43

1. Make the lining

With right sides facing, pin together the two bag lining pieces. Sew around the sides and bottom, leaving the top edge open.

2. Make the outside of the bag

Pleats first. Carefully pull the fabric in where each pleat is marked until you have a little pulled-up triangle of fabric. It should exactly match the pleat line you've marked on the fabric. Pin it just *outside* the line of the triangle. Now stitch along the marked line. Repeat for the other pleat. Hurrah – you've pleated!

Repeat the pleating for the other bag body piece.

With right sides facing, pin one bag body piece to one bag top piece. Sew together along the pinned edge. Repeat with the other bag body piece and the bag top piece. Remove the pins and press the seam flat towards the bag body.

With right sides facing, pin together these pieces that you've just made. Sew around the edges, again leaving the top edge open.

3. Make the handles

Fold the handle piece in half lengthways and press flat to create a line down the centre. Then fold each edge in to meet this centre line and press flat. Now fold the whole thing in half lengthways again and press flat. Stitch into place along each edge, as close to the edge as you can manage. Repeat for the other handle piece. There you go – you have two handles!

4. Put it all together

Make sure that the lining is *wrong* side out and the outer bag is *right* side out.

Fold over the top edge of the lining by about 5 mm onto the wrong side (the little folded bit that peeks over should be the printed side of the fabric; refer to the diagram). Press. Sew neatly all the way around the top.

Fold under 5 mm of the top edge of the outer bag and press it flat to create a neat edge. Sew neatly all the way around the top. The lining and the outer bag are now hemmed.

Insert the lining (still wrong side out) into the outer bag. Align the top edges neatly and push the lining down inside the bag and into the corners.

Position the handles, one on each side of the bag, making sure they are evenly spaced, the same length and not twisted. They need to be sandwiched between the outer bag and the lining so that the messy ends will be concealed. Pin them in place through all the layers of fabric. Double-check their placement and length.

Now sew all the way around the top of the bag (don't sew it closed!). You should be stitching through only three layers of fabric – the outside, the handle and the inside. Now sew around the top again to make it super-strong. You can use a straight stitch, or if your machine has any decorative stitches, this might be a good opportunity to give them a whirl.

Press your LOVELY bag and you are DONE!

pin & stitch

bag top

pleat → ← pleat

bag body

right side   wrong side

stitch into place

bag lining pieces

Custom-designed felt brooch

You can make a brooch from felt. You really can. You might make a cat, like this, or perhaps a simple bird or a sausage dog. Here's how to do it the easy-peasy way.

PROJECT BY: ANNA LAURA BLANDFORD
SUITABLE FOR: BEGINNERS
SHOULD TAKE: ABOUT 1 HOUR

SHOPPING LIST

◇ Felt – this project uses a really small amount of felt, so it is a great project for using up scraps and offcuts
◇ Badge back (with holes in it so you can stitch it onto the felt) – available from craft or sewing supply stores
◇ Polyester toy stuffing
◇ Embroidery floss in colours you like

CRAFTY NEEDS

◇ Thread and needle
◇ Small, sharp scissors

BEFORE YOU START SEWING

Do some drawings of possible ideas for your badge. Think about the different shapes in your design. Perhaps it's just a front and a back with some features stitched on. Or maybe you want to add other embellishments, such as wings, big floppy ears or wheels. It depends on what you are making. For inspiration, refer to children's books, old encyclopedias or things around you.

Once you have decided on your design, sketch out the shapes you will need to cut from the felt and also plan any stitched features. It's best to keep it simple, and to work it all out on paper first so you know exactly what you're doing before you start cutting.

Note that seam allowances are 5 mm, although as you're using felt, you may be able to get away with a little less.

1. Cut out your shapes

When you cut out your shape, make sure it is a wee bit bigger than you want the finished badge to be. This is because it will become three-dimensional, so the final stuffed shape will be smaller than the flat shape you start with.

Although it is quicker to cut the two layers of felt together, the results will be better if you cut one, then cut the other, using the first one as a guide. Be patient. If you find once you've sewn it up that one edge is longer, you can trim it off.

2. Attach the brooch back

Stitch the brooch back onto the right side of the back of your badge. It is best to do this first, before you start adding features and sewing it all together. Stitch through from the wrong side to keep your stitching neat. Be tidy and use tight stitches.

3. Adding details

On the right side of the front of the badge, sew on the details and any embellishments. Here's where you can stitch on eyes, a little nose, or whatever features your badge calls for. Double-check you're sewing onto the correct side by lining up your pieces – you don't want to accidentally stitch the face on the inside of the front piece. Heavens no!

If you are sewing on extra pieces of felt, a neat backstitch is recommended. It is super easy to do. Try to keep all your stitches the same length. Only use two strands of embroidery floss; this gives sharper details and a neater finish. The more you practise, the better you'll get. If you are feeling more adventurous or you're an embroidery supremo, you can use other styles of stitching.

4. Stitching it together

Once you've added all the details, match the back and front pieces with wrong sides facing, and stitch the back and the front together. Before you start stitching, work out where you will be inserting the stuffing, and start stitching from that point. Make sure the gap that you leave for the stuffing is in a nice, central area, and in a part of the design that is not too curvy or complicated.

Stitch the brooch closed with a basic running stitch, securing each end of stitching firmly so that it won't come undone once you insert the stuffing. Then stuff the brooch. If you have some small areas that are too hard to fill using fingers, use a long, thin object such as a knitting needle to gently push the filling up. Keep filling the badge until it looks firm, and then stitch the gap closed, making sure to finish the stitching so the ends of the threads don't show.

PIN ON and wear with a SMILE!

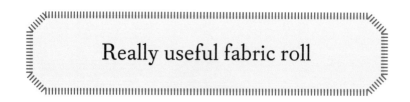

Really useful fabric roll

This fabric roll was designed to stow a multitude of important things, be they picnic cutlery, stationery or paintbrushes. This is a clever-clogs storage solution for the crafter on the move!

PROJECT BY: KATE HENDERSON
SUITABLE FOR: BEGINNERS
SHOULD TAKE: ABOUT 1 HOUR

SHOPPING LIST

◇ 30 cm × 60 cm piece of denim or heavy fabric
◇ 30 cm × 40 cm piece of contrasting cotton fabric
◇ 20 cm × 20 cm piece of double-sided iron-on interfacing (such as Vlicsofix or Thermoweb Heat and Bond)
◇ 75 cm ribbon about 1 cm wide

CRAFTY NEEDS

◇ Sewing machine
◇ Thread to match your fabric
◇ Paper scissors
◇ Fabric scissors
◇ Measuring tape or ruler
◇ Dressmaker's pins
◇ Iron
◇ Seam ripper in case of mistakes

PATTERN NEEDS

◇ There are three pattern pieces: body piece A, inside pocket piece B and appliqué piece C.
◇ Cut one body piece A in denim and one in cotton.
◇ Cut one inside pocket piece B in denim.
◇ To prepare the three appliqué pieces, first trace the appliqué piece C shape three times onto the papery side of the double-sided interfacing with a pen. Cut out each shape out roughly 1 cm outside the traced outline (you will cut it out neatly after you have ironed it on to the fabric).
◇ Iron this traced-on interfacing piece, shiny side down, onto the wrong side of the appliqué fabric. It will adhere with heat. Now it's time to cut neatly around the traced outline. Your appliqué shapes are now prepared and can later be ironed onto your fabric roll.

BEFORE YOU START SEWING

◇ Cut out the pieces and prepare the appliqué shapes as detailed above.
◇ Make sure your machine is threaded and your bobbin is full.
◇ Note that seam allowances are 1 cm unless it says otherwise.
◇ For best results, trim loose threads as you go.

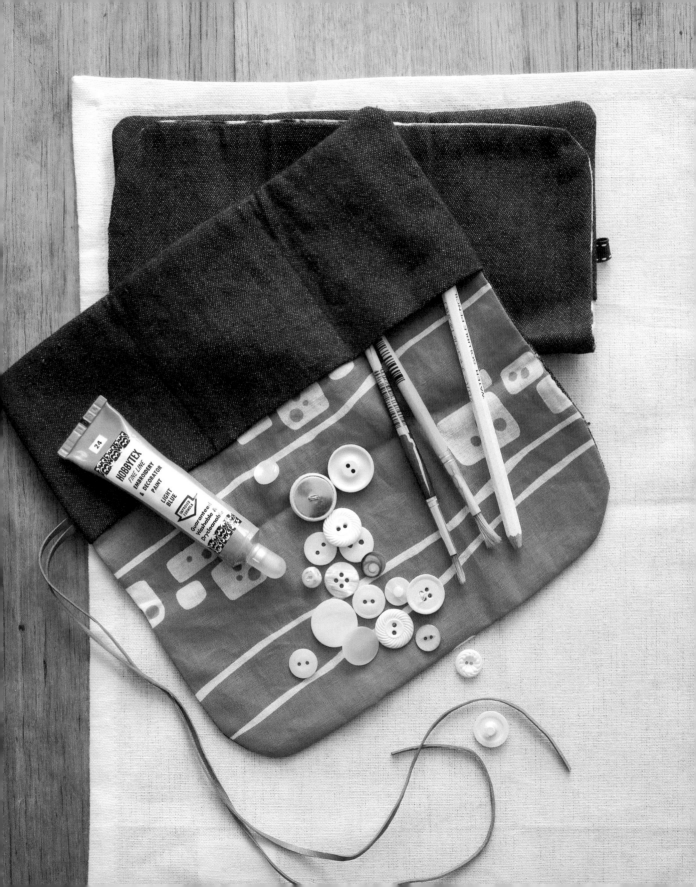

1. Appliqué first

Iron the prepared appliqué shapes onto the denim body piece A. To do this, peel the backing paper from the shape and position each shape where you would like it to be on the body piece. Play around until you're happy with the arrangement. Then iron each shape on until it has fused. This will only take a second or two. Now stitch around the edge of each shape in a straight or decorative stitch.

2. Make the inside of the roll

Fold the inside pocket piece B in half as marked and press well. With right sides together, pin edge A to the bottom of the cotton body piece A. Put a couple of pins in each side too. Sew down the two lines (as marked on the pattern) to begin to form the pockets.

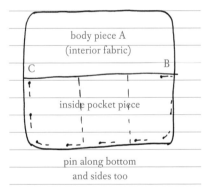

pin along bottom
and sides too

3. Attach the ribbon

Cut the ribbon in half and, with the two ribbon pieces right sides facing, pin to point B on the right-hand edge of the outside body piece A, on the right side of the fabric. It needs to lie flat across the body piece as shown in the diagram. To prevent it from being sewn into the seam later, fold it up a few times and pin it in the middle of the body piece, as shown.

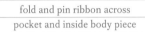

fold and pin ribbon across
pocket and inside body piece

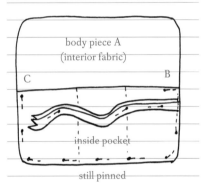

still pinned

4. Sew it all together

Remove the pins from bottom edge and sides. With right sides together, pin the outside and inside body pieces together. The ribbon should be sandwiched in the middle. Pin all around the edges, then sew the seam, remembering to leave an opening for turning out as marked on the pattern.

5. Finish it off

Turn the roll right side out and press flat. You have two options for finishing the roll. You can machine topstitch around the top part of the fabric roll, from point B up and around to point C. This will finish the roll nicely and sew up the still-open gap in the side seam. Or just hand sew the gap closed using tiny, strong stitches in a thread to match the fabric.

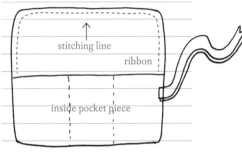

stitch around top to finish

Fold down the top of the roll, roll into thirds and tie up. Now think about the lovely and useful things you might pop into it!

Flower and bird coasters

This is a lovely project for beginning sewers. You will learn how to appliqué and embroider, and you can put your own stamp on these coasters with your favourite fabrics and some clever stitching. Tiel is a wonderful illustrator, and it really shines through in her project.

PROJECT BY: **TIEL SEIVL-KEEVERS**
SUITABLE FOR: **BEGINNERS**
SHOULD TAKE: **ABOUT 1 HOUR**

SHOPPING LIST

◇ 30 cm × 60 cm piece of natural-coloured linen or cotton for the coasters
◇ Small scraps of printed cotton for the appliqué
◇ Embroidery floss in your favourite colours if you intend to hand stitch
◇ Thread to match the linen
◇ Contrasting thread if you are going to do machine embroidery

CRAFTY NEEDS

◇ Sewing machine
◇ Paper scissors
◇ Fabric scissors, or rotary cutter and cutting mat
◇ Ruler
◇ Dressmaker's pins (or appliqué pins if you have them)
◇ Iron
◇ Seam ripper in case of mistakes
◇ Air-fading fabric marker or tailor's chalk
◇ Chopstick or knitting needle for turning out
◇ Double-sided iron-on interfacing (such as Vliesofix or Thermoweb Heat and Bond)
◇ Dressmaker's carbon paper

PATTERN NEEDS

From the linen or cotton main fabric, cut eight pieces of fabric each measuring 12 cm × 12 cm. You can make your own pattern piece to this size and cut around it, or use a ruler to draw lines on the fabric with fading fabric marker or tailor's chalk. Alternatively, use a rotary cutter and mat if you have them.

BEFORE YOU START SEWING

◇ Cut out the pattern pieces as detailed above.
◇ Make sure your machine is threaded and your bobbin is full.
◇ Note that seam allowances are 5 mm unless it says otherwise.
◇ Sew each seam twice to stop fraying and add strength.
◇ For best results, trim loose threads as you go.
◇ Try to persuade someone to put a big pot of soup on the stove so you can pop your soup-filled mugs on these coasters later!

First, decide whether you want to embroider, appliqué or both.

1. Appliquéd bird

Draw the solid appliqué bird outline onto the papery side of the double-sided interfacing. Cut around this roughly, a centimetre or two bigger than the traced outline. Put this shape, shiny side down (that's the adhesive side), onto the wrong side of your chosen contrast fabric scrap. Press with a hot iron so it adheres. Now cut out the bird shape neatly, exactly on the outline. Peel off the backing paper and iron this appliqué piece, sticky side down, onto one of the linen squares. Sew around the outside of the bird by hand or by machine.

2. Appliquéd flower

Use the same technique as above.

3. Embroidered flower

Transfer the flower outline onto the linen. To do this, draw the design on a piece of ordinary paper, then place the carbon paper over the fabric piece, carbon side down, and position it carefully. Put the flower outline over the carbon paper, and, using the end of a knitting needle or similar, trace around the outline to transfer it.

Stitch around the outline by machine or by hand. You can use a running stitch, backstitch or whatever stitch you like.

4. Embroidered bird

Follow the same steps as for the embroidered flower.

5. Other decorative touches

You can use your sewing machine to add more decorative stitches, some borders or even your own designs. A little leaf or heart or some text might be nice.

6. Finish the coasters

Be sure that at least four of the squares have been embroidered or appliquéd. If you embellish only four of them, they will have plain backing squares. If you embellish all eight of them, the coasters will be reversible.

With right sides facing, match one embellished coaster square to one backing square and pin. Sew around each square 5 mm from the edge, leaving a 5 cm opening along one side for turning out. Trim any excess fabric before turning out, and snip the corners of each coaster close to the stitching at a 45-degree angle. Turn out, using a chopstick or knitting needle to push the corners right out. Press, then neatly hand sew the opening closed using tiny stitches.

Nice work! Won't your tabletop look lovely now?

Made-to-measure vintage obi and skirt/halter top

The story of a rectangle in two parts: A reversible obi belt and a skirt
that moonlights as a halter top – made just to fit you!

PROJECT BY: NANETTE LOUCHART-FLETCHER
SUITABLE FOR: BEGINNERS
SHOULD TAKE: ABOUT 2 HOURS

SHOPPING LIST

For the skirt/top:

◇ 60 cm × 120 cm piece of fabric (we used a vintage
   curtain, but you could use any lovely printed cotton)
◇ 2 cm-wide elastic, long enough to fit your waist plus
◇ 3 cm for overlap
◇ 1 m of 6 mm binding for the strap, if you want to also
   wear the skirt as a top (this binding can match or
   contrast with your skirt, depending on your preference.
   Or you could use ribbon or other trim instead of binding)
◇ Large safety pin
◇ 10 cm × 30 cm piece of cardboard

For the obi:

◇ 1 metre of main fabric (patterned or plain – your choice)
◇ About ten different scraps of fabric in a complementary
   colour palette for each side (for a reversible obi, you will
   need about 20 scraps)
◇ Piece of cardboard for the templates, at least 50 cm wide
   and as long as your waist measurement
◇ 2 m of 6-mm binding, ribbon or other trim that can be tied
◇ 25 cm of low-loft batting at least 60 cm wide

CRAFTY NEEDS

◇ Sewing machine
◇ Thread to match or contrast with your fabric
◇ Paper scissors
◇ Fabric scissors, or rotary cutter and cutting mat
◇ Measuring tape
◇ Ruler
◇ Dressmaker's pins
◇ Iron and ironing board
◇ Seam ripper in case of mistakes

BEFORE YOU START SEWING

◇ Make sure your machine is threaded and your bobbin
   is full.
◇ Note that seam allowances are 1 cm unless it says
   otherwise.
◇ For best results, trim loose threads as you go.
◇ Take the 10 cm × 30 cm piece of cardboard and rule
   lines across the longest side at the 5 mm, 1 cm, 1.5 cm
   and 4 cm points. This is a genius method for pressing
   seam allowances and skipping the tedium of pins.
◇ An excellent get-you-in-the-sewing-mood mixtape
   would be a good idea right now!

1. Make your skirt

Fold in 1 cm along both short edges of the fabric and press. Fold in and press 1 cm more to make a double hem that will catch and hide your raw seams. Sew with a 5 mm seam allowance. This will keep the side seams of your skirt super neat.

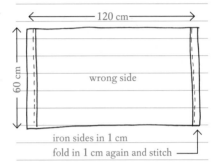

Next, fold in 1 cm along the top edge of the fabric and press. Fold in 4 cm more along the same edge and press. This will form a casing to thread your elastic through for the waistband of your skirt.

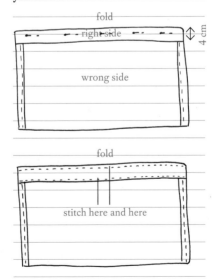

Stitch two parallel lines along the waistband to make the casing as shown. The first line is 1 cm from the folded top. The second line is 5 mm from the bottom of the waistband.

Now give some thought to the length of your skirt. Stand in front of the mirror with your fabric, experimenting with different lengths to determine what works best for you. Trim your fabric to about 1.5 cm below your desired length to allow for the hem.

With the wrong side facing you, fold up 5 mm along this bottom edge. Press. Fold up 1 cm more to conceal the raw edge. Press again, then sew this hem into place.

Now it's time to sew it together! With right sides facing, fold the rectangle of fabric in half widthways. Starting at the bottom hem, sew the side seam with a 1.5 cm seam allowance. Stop sewing when you are 1 cm away from the base of the waistband.

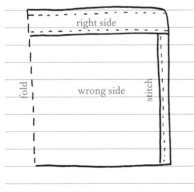

If you haven't already done so, measure the elastic around your waist to work out how much you need. Add an extra 2.5 cm or so. Pin the large safety pin to one end of the elastic and slip it inside the casing on the waistband. Push it along, bunching up the casing fabric as you go, until the pin comes out the other end of the casing. Do this carefully so the elastic does not twist. Also make sure the loose end of the elastic does not disappear into the casing.

Consider whether you intend to wear the skirt also as a halter neck. If so, try it on at your bustline and make additional adjustments so it is comfortable as both a skirt and a top. Using a narrow zig-zag stitch, sew the ends of your elastic together securely, going back and forth a few times. Tuck the join into the casing. You can stitch the opening closed, or leave it open if you prefer.

2. Make it a halter too!

If you intend to wear it as a halter top, try it on and use four pins to mark the two points where you would like the straps to be. Take the 6-mm binding and measure the length required for the straps to sit comfortably around your neck, allowing about 4 cm extra for overlap on the inside of the top. Cut the binding and sew by hand or machine (I prefer hand sewing for this part) to the points marked.

You're done. You made a skirt (and halter too!). Pour yourself a beverage of choice and get on with making the obi.

3. Make the obi

Make the ties

Press the binding piece in half length-ways and machine sew all the way along to secure. Cut into four pieces each 50 cm long and knot one end of each piece. Your ties are done!

Make your template

Measure your waistline. Use this measurement as the basis for the width template – be aware that this will give you a belt that's a few centimetres smaller than your template on each side due to seams. That's okay, as it's not meant to fit you exactly, just decoratively. Also, it sits open a few inches at the back, so it needs to be a few inches smaller than your waist.

Decide how long you would like your obi to be. Cut two rectangular templates in cardboard to these measurements. For example, ours measured 70 cm (width) x 18 cm (length). You will use these cardboard templates as the pattern for your obi 'patchwork'.

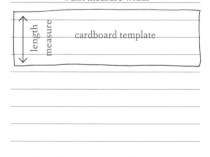

Make the first side of the obi

Now's the fun part. Cut one of the templates into four or five horizontal strips in varying widths and with proportions that are pleasing to your eye. If you are not completely happy, cut another template and try again. Explore and experiment! When you are happy with your horizontal strips, it's time to cut them vertically too at random points.

Use these template pieces as your guide for cutting the patched strips of your main fabric and your complimentary scrap fabrics. Refer to the photo for inspiration. Collect all the pieces for each width of strip into a separate pile and then reassemble the strips one at a time. Lay the pieces out on a flat surface and move them around until you have an arrangement that pleases you. Then sew each strip together.

Stitch your strips together to form one side of the obi. The finished strips need to match the size of the uncut rectangle template when stitched together. Trim to the correct size with a rotary cutter or scissors.

Make the second side of the obi

Repeat the above procedure, mixing up the strips again until you are super happy with the look of your obi.

Sew the batting, obi and ties together

Form the 'sandwich' layers of your belt. Place one obi piece right side up. Attach two binding strips to each end as shown, facing them inwards and aligning the unknotted ends with the edge of the obi piece. These will form the belt ties. Secure them with pins. Place the other obi piece on top of this, right side facing down. Measure the finished obi and cut a piece of low-loft batting to this size. Lay the batting on top of the obi pieces. Pin the whole sandwich together.

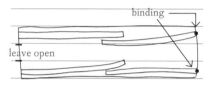

Sew around the sides of the batting/ obi sandwich with a 1 cm seam allowance, leaving one end open as shown. Remove the pins and trim the raw edges to within 2 mm of the seam. Carefully clip the corners at a 45-degree angle. Gently turn the belt out the right way, using a large knitting needle to slowly and gently push out the corners to a point. Do not push too hard, as you risk tearing the fabric and having to make a massive donation to the swear jar.

Tuck the unfinished edge inside and hand stitch this edge closed. Trim all threads and press the obi, then you're done. Try the whole lot on in front of a mirror and love yourself sick for being both clever and gorgeous.

Zing the polite cat

This adorable kitty won't scratch the legs of your chic-teak dining table any time soon.
He will, however, sit quietly while you catch up on your email or a spot of craft blogging.
He's a sweet companion for anyone with a softie soft spot.

PROJECT BY: JHOANNA MONTE ARANEZ
SUITABLE FOR: SOFTIE-LOVING BEGINNERS
SHOULD TAKE: 2 TO 3 HOURS

SHOPPING LIST

◇ 50 cm × 70 cm piece of heavy fabric (such as denim or wool) for the body
◇ 20 cm × 20 cm piece of printed cotton for the belly
◇ 20 cm × 20 cm piece of tan felt for the face
◇ 15 cm × 15 cm piece of black felt for the eyes and nose
◇ 20 cm of colourful ric-rac trim
◇ Embroidery floss in black and white
◇ Black thread
◇ Polyester or wool toy stuffing

CRAFTY NEEDS

◇ Sewing machine
◇ Paper scissors
◇ Fabric scissors
◇ Measuring tape or ruler
◇ Iron
◇ Dressmaker's pins (or appliqué pins if you have them)
◇ Chopstick or knitting needle for turning out
◇ Seam ripper in case of mistakes

PATTERN NEEDS

There are seven pattern pieces: body, face, belly, arm, leg, eye and nose. Cut as follows:
◇ From the heavy fabric, cut two body pieces.
◇ From the heavy fabric, cut two arm pieces.
◇ From the heavy fabric, cut two leg pieces.
◇ From the heavy fabric, cut two back pieces.
◇ From the printed cotton, cut one belly piece.
◇ From the tan felt, cut one face piece.
◇ From the black felt, cut two eyes.
◇ From the black felt, cut one nose.

BEFORE YOU START SEWING

◇ Cut out the pattern pieces as detailed above.
◇ Make sure your machine is threaded and your bobbin is full.
◇ Note that seam allowances are 1 cm unless it says otherwise.
◇ Sew each seam twice to stop fraying and add strength.
◇ For best results, trim loose threads as you go.
◇ Trim the seams and clip along the curves to give them a nicer shape once they are turned right side out and stuffed.

1. First, the face

Pin the felt face piece onto the right side of the body piece as marked on the pattern. You can hand stitch it using blanket stitch, or use the sewing machine and a straight stitch or zig-zag. Make it as neat as you can.

Now for the features. Position the eyes and nose pieces, secure with pins and stitch into place by hand or machine. Embroider a tiny line in the top right-hand corner of each eye as shown on the pattern to add expression. Backstitch would be the perfect stitch to use here. Embroider some eyebrows, a mouth and whiskers as shown, again using backstitch. Use the photo of lovely Zing as a guide. Make him look cute.

2. Make the body, hands and arms

Pin the belly piece onto the right side of Zing's front body piece as marked on the pattern. Sew it into place, in the same way you did with the face piece previously. Good work!

Take one pair of matching arm pieces. With right sides facing, pin them together, then sew along the curved edge, leaving the top of the arm open to allow for stuffing. Do the same with the other arm pieces. Remember the trim and clip the curved seams. Turn the arms right side out and use a chopstick or knitting needle to push out all the curves and corners. Press flat with the iron. There you go – super-flat cat arms!

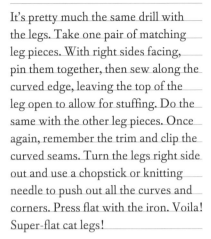

It's pretty much the same drill with the legs. Take one pair of matching leg pieces. With right sides facing, pin them together, then sew along the curved edge, leaving the top of the leg open to allow for stuffing. Do the same with the other leg pieces. Once again, remember the trim and clip the curved seams. Turn the legs right side out and use a chopstick or knitting needle to push out all the curves and corners. Press flat with the iron. Voila! Super-flat cat legs!

Machine or hand sew small lines of stitching on the arms and legs to make cute paws, referring to the photo as a guide.

Stuff each arm and leg until firm, being sure that the stuffing is nice and even. Just take your time with this and use small pieces of stuffing to get a 'firm stuff'. (Using bits of stuffing that are too big can make the limbs look lumpy.) Use the chopstick or the knitting needle to get the stuffing right down into the ends. When you're happy, stitch the open end of each arm and leg closed. Don't worry about being too neat, as this stitching will be concealed inside the body pieces later.

3. Put it all together

Place Zing's front down on a table, right side up. Position the arms and legs as indicated on the diagram, with all limbs evenly placed and pointing in across the body. Be sure the pieces sit nicely with their edges lined up with the edge of the body piece. Take note of where the stitching is on the ends of the arm and leg pieces so you can sew *just* inside it to conceal it. Pin all the bits into place. Don't worry if the paws are all on top of each other at this stage.

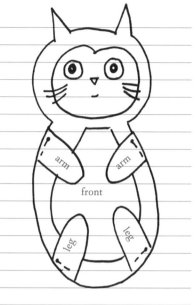

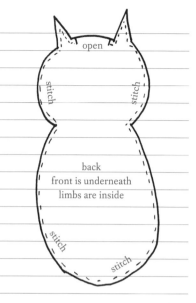

Tuck limbs in and pin to front piece.
Next, put back of Zing on top
(right side down) and stitch around
body edge as per instructions.

Sew around the edge, leaving a gap between the ears, as indicated on the pattern piece, for turning out and stuffing later. Then sew around the body again for good measure and extra strength.

Carefully trim all the seams and clip any curves so they will sit flat. Carefully snip the top off the ear seams – but don't cut the stitching!

Turn Zing the right way out. Again, use the knitting needle or chopstick to poke all the curves and corners out. Press flat.

Stuff with small pieces of stuffing, starting at the bottom of the body and working your way up. This ensures that he's not lumpy. (If he's lumpy, you are stuffing him with big bits again. Stop that.) When he's nice and firm and evenly stuffed, sew him closed using a tiny ladder stitch.

Sew his ric-rac tail on and knot the end.

FINISHED!
Give him a hug,
or let him watch
you blog.
HE LIKES THAT.

Yoga pants for happy babies

The weeny person's downward dog will be so much more adorable in these made-by-you pants. This is a super-simple project kindly designed for the beginning sewer. Shannon designed and printed the fabric for these pants. A bought or vintage fabric is the easy way to go, or you could get extra crafty and use the instructions on page 48 to screenprint a personalised design.

PROJECT BY: SHANNON LAMDEN
SUITABLE FOR: CAREFUL, PATIENT BEGINNERS
SHOULD TAKE: NO MORE THAN 1 ½ HOURS

SHOPPING LIST

◇ 50 cm of printed cotton fabric 112–115 cm wide
◇ 35 cm of elastic, about 1 cm wide

CRAFTY NEEDS

◇ Sewing machine
◇ Thread to match your fabric
◇ Paper scissors
◇ Fabric scissors
◇ Measuring tape
◇ Dressmaker's pins
◇ Iron
◇ Seam ripper in case of mistakes
◇ Large safety pin

PATTERN NEEDS

There is one pattern piece.
Cut it out twice on the fold of the fabric.

BEFORE YOU START SEWING

◇ Cut out the pattern pieces as indicated.
◇ Make sure your machine is threaded and your bobbin is full.
◇ Note that seam allowances are 1 cm unless it says otherwise.
◇ Sew each seam twice to stop fraying and add strength.
◇ For best results, trim loose threads as you go.
◇ If you don't use an overlocker, it's best to zig-zag over the raw edges of each seam with your sewing machine to finish them nicely.

NOTE

These will fit a baby aged 9–12 months. If you have a baby on hand, adjust the length of the pants to suit.

Pattern #. 21043

Blocks b

ronyounee!

1. Sew the pieces together

Open out the two folded pieces and pin them together – with the right sides facing. Sew along both outside leg seams (A) first. Then, sew along the inside leg seam (B) all the way from one side to the other (there's only one long curved seam here). Sew this crotch seam again to reinforce.

2. Hem the legs

Now you've formed the legs of the pants. Still keeping the wrong side facing out, fold up the hem of each leg 1 cm. Press. Fold up another 1 cm. Press again. Make sure the legs are the same length. Stitch around the bottom of each leg to form the hem. (Be careful not to stitch the front and the back of the leg together – keep the rest of the leg fabric pulled well away from where you are stitching.)

3. Create the waistband

Fold the top of the pants down 1 cm. Press. Fold it down another 2 cm. Press again. Pin to secure. You need to stitch along the bottom of this folded bit (about 1.7 cm down from the top of the pants) to form the waistband and to create a casing to thread the elastic through. Don't sew all the way along – you need to leave a gap of about 1.5 cm at the end of the stitching so you can insert your elastic.

At this stage the pants are still the wrong way out.

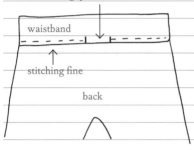

leave gap to thread elastic

waistband

stitching fine

back

cup C

4. Thread the elastic

Attach the safety pin to the elastic and push it into the little gap you left, and thread it through the casing. Keep pushing, bunching up the fabric, until the safety pin comes out the other end. Don't let go of the other end of the elastic or it might disappear into the casing never to be seen again! Pull the safety pin back out of the gap and machine sew the two ends of the elastic together securely. For super strength, use a small zig-zag and sew back and forth a few times.

Now push the join in the elastic up into the casing – the end of a pencil can help with this. Stitch up the gap you left, pulling the elastic taut as you go so your stitches aren't all bunchy.

You made 'em! Turn the pants the right way out and press. Then find the cutest baby you can to model them.

Ephemera mobile

This beautiful mobile can be customised to suit your own collection of bits and pieces. I think it's the perfect, ever-changing inspiration installation. Make this with your own collection of special things and it will be unique.

PROJECT BY: MARIANNE HORTON
SUITABLE FOR: BEGINNERS
SHOULD TAKE: ABOUT 2 HOURS, PLUS DRYING TIME

SHOPPING LIST

◊ Wire coat hanger or 1 m of similar-gauge wire
◊ String to cover mobile frame
◊ Linen thread or twine for stringing and hanging
◊ Small ring, hook or similar fixture from which to suspend mobile
◊ PVC glue
◊ Masking tape
◊ Gloss or matt gel medium
◊ Things to hang, such as sheet music, old book pages, gift cards or your choice of paper or thin card, metallic thread, embroidery floss, beads, tiny toys, costume jewellery, old lace doilies, an assortment of buttons and any other ephemera that you might wish to use
◊ Cotton tape or ribbon

CRAFTY NEEDS

◊ Paper scissors
◊ Measuring tape
◊ Dressmaker's pins
◊ Hair dryer (optional)
◊ Sharp needle (with an eye big enough for your linen thread or twine)
◊ Waxed paper
◊ Wire cutters or heavy-duty scissors

PATTERN NEEDS

We have provided leaf templates to trace on this page 107. You will find the instructions for making the paper flowers on page 107.

BEFORE YOU START

Organise a nice, clear, well-ventilated work space. Cut out the leaves and make the flowers as detailed overleaf.

1. Prepare the paper and lace

For protection and durability, you need to coat the paper and lace. Just lay them out on a waxed-paper-protected surface and paint a liberal coat of gel medium over each piece of paper and lace. Leave to dry naturally (or use a hair dryer).

2. Make the mobile frame

Use the wire cutters to cut the hook from the coat hanger, just below the twisted base. Straighten the hanger out as much as you can and then bend it into a circular shape to whatever size you please. Make sure you leave an overlap of at least 3 cm at the ends.

Use masking tape to secure the overlapped ends. Don't worry that it looks ugly – you'll be covering it up next! Starting a few centimetres past the overlap, coat a portion of wire with some PVC glue and start wrapping the wire frame with a length of string. Continue glueing and wrapping until the string effect is as thick as you would like. Secure the ends well with more glue. Next, paint over the string again with PVC glue to make it extra strong – the glue will dry clear. (You can also use more thread to wrap and embellish the ring.)

Now, referring to the diagrams below, cut two 60-cm lengths of string. Take the hanging ring and attach each piece of string to the ring at the 30 cm mark, tying a knot firmly. Do the same with the other length of string. Now you need to tie these four ends to four points on your wrapped wire frame so that the frame hangs evenly suspended.

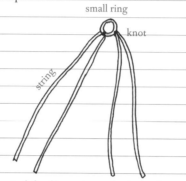

attach 2 x 60 cm pieces of string to ring at halfway point to make 4 lengths as shown

large string wrapped wire ring

You can further decorate it with anything you like: metallic thread, buttons randomly woven onto the frame, or any found objects such as old bits of costume jewellery, watch parts, small toys, beads or shells. Hunt, scavenge, imagine and improvise.

3. Make the hanging strings

Take your assortment of pieces to hang and thread a sharp needle with a length of linen thread or twine. Make it whatever length you like plus an extra 30 cm, which you can trim back later to get the effect you want. Thread your selected objects onto the linen thread. Loosely tie or position your threaded pieces at varying lengths and positions on the mobile – it's easiest to do this with the frame hanging so it's all nice and even and you can see the final effect. You may want to play around with the length, position and balance. Try to ensure that the frame hangs straight. Add as many adorned lengths as you like. Knot the lengths to secure and trim the ends. Buttons or beads threaded at the end of each string will help with the final 'hang'.

When it looks the way that you like, you're done. Hang it up in a breezy window and admire it while sipping something delicious!

Paper flower instructions

Cut paper strip
(12 mm × 140 mm approximately
or to desired size).

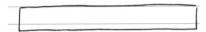

Fold and secure with needle
and thread (tie knot in end).

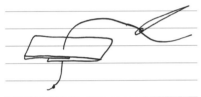

Continue making and adding strips
until flower is desired size.

Finish with a button, paper loop
or gathered cotton tape, as desired.

Leaf template

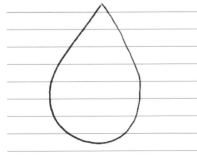

Cut paper strips
(12 mm × 140 mm and
10 mm × 100 mm approximately
or to desired size).

Continue making and adding strips
until flower is desired size.

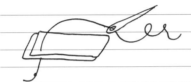

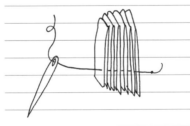

Pass thread back through first two or
three strips to secure and complete
flower shape. Finish with a button or
paper loop.

Cut paper strips
(12 mm × 140 mm and
10 mm × 100 mm approximately
or to desired size).

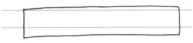

Large strips:
Fold and secure with needle and
thread (tie knot in end).

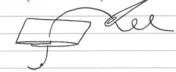

Small strips:
Do not fold, pass thread through
center of flat strip.

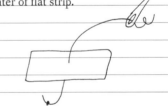

Continue making and adding strips
until flower is desired size. Finish with
a button and small paper loop.

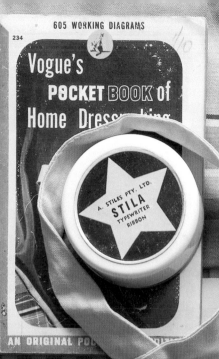

605 WORKING DIAGRAMS

234

Vogue's
POCKET BOOK of
Home Dressmaking

AN ORIGINAL POC...

A. STILES PTY. LTD.
STILA
TYPEWRITER
RIBBON

THE SLUMBERING FAIRIES

Eight Little
Fairy Tales

WITH WORDS
for
PIANO SOLO
by
MAE AILEEN ERB
Op. 15

(FROM WOOD ED. 755)

No. 1. Just Because It's You
No. 2. Sing, Little Bird
No. 3. The Moon Boat
No. 4. The Grey Squirrel
No. 5. The Fairy Boatman
No. 6. The Lonesome Apple
No. 7. The Little Brook
No. 8. The Slumbering Fairies

PRICE, 1/3.

Copyright B. F. Wood Music Co., Boston, U.S.A.

NICHOLSON'S PTY. LTD.
"The Musical Centre," 416 GEORGE ST., SYDNEY.

T
2A

L.S.G.
SUNBEAMS

L.S.G.
SUNBEAMS

L.S.G.
SUNBEAMS

bits and bobs

7♣ 3♦

2♥ ♠6

🍎🍎🍎 🍎🍎🍎🍎🍎

8 = 3 + 5 = 6 + ▢

9 = 3 + 6 = 2 + ▢

2:16

Fabric backgammon board

This is guaranteed to be the craftiest game of backgammon you have ever played – and I'm not talking strategy! It's a great beginner's quilting project that will teach you all the basics.

PROJECT BY: LEAH CHAPMAN
SUITABLE FOR: AMBITIOUS BEGINNERS
SHOULD TAKE: NO MORE THAN 5 HOURS (THE EMBROIDERY AND BINDING WILL TAKE THE MOST TIME - BUT IT'S WORTH IT. YOU'LL JUST NEED SOME TEA AND BISCUITS TO HELP YOU THROUGH)

SHOPPING LIST

◇ 50 cm × 50 cm piece of plain light-coloured cotton or cotton–linen fabric (Fabric 1)
◇ 20 cm × 40 cm piece of contrasting printed cotton print (Fabric 2)
◇ 50 cm × 50 cm piece of printed cotton for the backing (Fabric 3)
◇ 50 cm × 50 cm piece of cotton batting
◇ 2 m of 2.5-cm wide red bias binding
◇ 45 cm of red ric-rac
◇ Embroidery floss in red and black
◇ Super-cheap but nice backgammon set
◇ Piece of thick cardboard to make the triangle template

CRAFTY NEEDS

Sewing machine
White thread
Bright thread in a contrasting colour
Paper scissors
Fabric scissors
Measuring tape or ruler
Dressmaker's pins
Iron
Seam ripper in case of mistakes
Air-fading fabric marker or tailor's chalk
Needle
Tracing paper or baking paper for tracing

PATTERN NEEDS

There are two pattern pieces.
◇ From Fabric 1, cut two of piece A.
◇ From Fabric 2, cut one of piece B.
Put Fabric 3 and the batting to one side until later.

BEFORE YOU START SEWING

◇ Cut out the pieces as detailed above.
◇ Make sure your machine is threaded and your bobbin is full.
◇ Note that seam allowances are 1 cm unless it says otherwise.
◇ For best results, trim loose threads as you go.

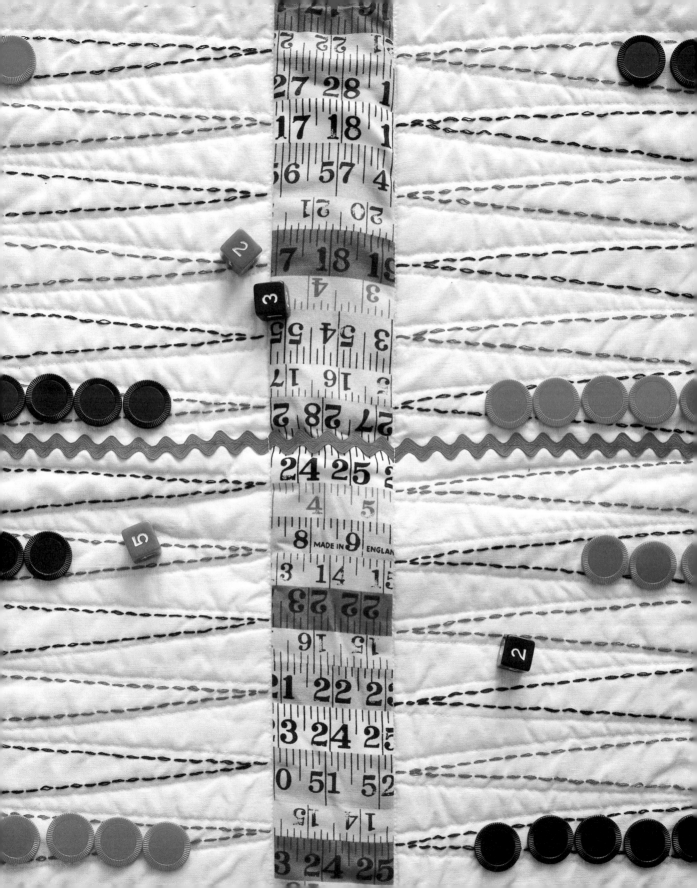

1. Make the template

Trace the triangle template on page 113 onto tracing paper or baking paper. Tape to the thick cardboard and cut out around the outline. You should now have one thick cardboard triangle suitable to trace around later.

2. Sew the front of the board

With right sides together, pin piece B to piece A along the longest side. Stitch in place about 5 mm from the edge. Attach the other piece A to the other long edge of piece B in the same way. You now have the three front pieces sewn together. Press all the seams flat.

Lay the sewn-together piece in front of you, right side up and with the patterned middle panel running horizontally. Excellent work.

3. Attach the ric-rac to the board

Find the centre of your piece by folding the fabric in half (from left over to right). Press this centre fold. Pin the ric-rac along this centre line and stitch into place. You should now have a board divided into four segments by the ric-rac strip and the fabric strip criss-crossing each other.

4. The embroidery is next

Press your board piece nice and flat. Using the template triangle, transfer the backgammon board outline to each quarter of the fabric board using tailor's chalk or an air-fading fabric marker. Refer to the photo as a guide. Note that you need to draw the design right up close to the ric-rac so that the stitching doesn't get 'lost' in the edges when you bind the board later with bias binding.

Next, embroider each triangle in running stitch in alternating colours, following the colour chart provided. Embroider with a fairly long stitch – about 7 mm long is good. Refer to the photo for guidance. When complete, press on the wrong side to flatten.

5. Now attach the batting

Don't be scared of batting – it's all froth. You need to cut one piece of batting and one piece of Fabric 3, both slightly larger than the game-board piece of fabric. Sandwich the batting between the backing and the game board. To do this, put Fabric 3 on the work surface, right side down, then the batting on top, then the embroidered right side of the board facing up. This is just how the board will be when it's finished, but with binding around the edges for extra neatness.

To keep all the layers together, you need to tack them in place. To do this, sew nice, long (about 3 cm) stitches in a star formation, working from the very centre out, through all the layers.

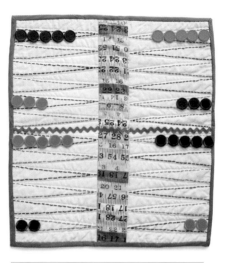

If you use a brightly coloured thread it will help when you take them out later. Don't worry about neatness, as these stitches are only temporary. The tacking will help the pieces to stay perfectly flat and bump-free. No-one likes a bumpy game board! Iron as you go if necessary.

6. It's time for the quilting part

Don't be scared of quilting either – it's just stitches! To quilt your board, machine sew using a straight stitch along the outline of the triangles, about 5 mm outside the embroidered line. It will look gorgeous. I promise. And it's easy peasy.

Trim the loose threads. Next, machine sew a neat, straight rectangle around the edge of the whole game board to secure the batting and the fabric layers together at the edges. Sew as close to the edge as you can, while still stitching through all the layers. Now trim the excess batting and backing from the edges to form a neat, even rectangular piece. Now bind the edges.

7. Binding

The following instructions might look long, but they're not complicated. Don't be put off – give it a go! Just take it step by step, punctuated with a nice cup of tea, and all will soon become clear. And you will have learnt a really useful craft skill!

Open out one of the folded edges of the bias binding. Beginning in the middle of one side of the back of the game board, pin the raw edge of this bias binding to the unfinished edge of the game board. The right side of the bias binding should be facing the back of the board. (The other folded edge of the bias binding will still be folded up, waiting to be unfolded and sewn later.)

Machine sew about 5mm in from the edge, all the way along, until you are 5 mm from the corner. Remove the work from the sewing machine, snip the threads and fold the binding as follows (refer to the diagrams as a guide).

To make the corner, fold the binding up at a 90-degree angle as shown. Finger-press and hold in place. The right side of the loose end of the binding will be facing you.

Colour template

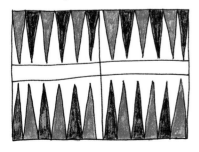

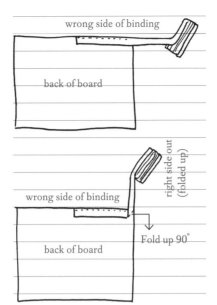

wrong side of binding

back of board

right side out (folded up)

wrong side of binding

back of board

Fold up 90°

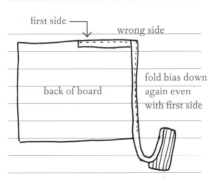

first side

wrong side

back of board

fold bias down again even with first side

3. Then fold the binding back down again so that the fold is level with the raw edges along the top of the work (the part you have just sewn along), and the raw edge of the loose end of the binding is level with the right-hand edge that will be sewn next. Now the wrong side of the binding will be facing you again. Pin into place. Now continue stitching along the next side, 5 mm from the edge as before. Repeat this process at each corner until you almost reach the point where you started binding.

8. Finish the binding

Turn the bound corners out and into place. Press flat. Hand sew the binding down on the other side (the non-embroidered side) with tiny invisible stitches all the way around until the whole thing is neat and nicely bound. Finish the ends by tucking under neatly and hand stitching.

Triangle template

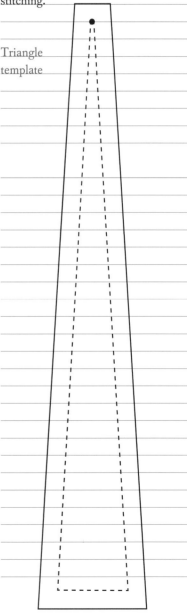

Chevron clutch

An amazing Noro yarn accentuates the chevron pattern in this lovely knitted clutch purse.
For this pattern, you will need to know how to knit, purl, cast on and cast off,
and how to sew up using backstitch or mattress stitch.

PROJECT BY: KYLIE ROBSON
SUITABLE FOR: CAREFUL, PATIENT BEGINNERS
SHOULD TAKE: ABOUT 1 HOUR

SHOPPING LIST

◇ 2 skeins (each 50 g) of Noro Silk Garden yarn
   (shown in shade 211)
◇ 4 mm needles, or size needed to obtain correct gauge
   (see Note)
◇ 30 cm × 50 cm piece of lining fabric
◇ 1 large decorative button
◇ 1 large sew-on press stud

CRAFTY NEEDS

◇ Sewing machine and thread
◇ Scissors
◇ Measuring tape or ruler
◇ Iron
◇ Yarn needle (one with a blunt tip) for finishing ends

ABBREVIATIONS

K2tog   Knit 2 stitches together, thus decreasing one stitch
kf&b   Knit into the front and back of the stitch before
        slipping it off the needle, thus increasing one stitch
sl1   Slip one stitch from the left-hand needle to the right-
        hand needle without knitting it. You usually knit
        the next stitch, and follow it with psso (see below)
psso   Pass the slipped stitch over the knitted stitch that
        has followed it
RS   Right side of the knitting
WS   Wrong side of the knitting

NOTE

If this is the first time you've tried knitting, see How to
Knit on page 134.

Gauge: 22 sts for each 10 cm in chevron stitch.
The 4 mm needles used for this project are slightly
smaller than those recommended on the yarn ball band,
because you need a firmer fabric to withstand use as a
clutch bag. Use whatever needles you need to obtain a
knitted tension of 22 sts over 10 cm in chevron stitch.

1. How to knit the chevron stitch pattern

The pattern goes like this:

Row 1 (RS) *K2tog, K2, kf&b in each of next 2 stitches, K3, sl1, K1, psso; rep from * to end of row.

Row 2 (WS) Purl.

2. Let's begin!

Cast on 110 sts. Knit one row (this is the right side).
Purl the next row (this is the wrong side).

Now, begin working in chevron stitch, starting with Row 1 of the chevron stitch pattern as detailed above. Continue until you have worked 25 cm, or the desired length, finishing with a right side (knit) row.

3. Cast off

Cast off, cut the yarn and fasten off, leaving at least 15 cm of excess yarn so you can weave the ends in nicely.

3. Weave in ends and sew knitted sides and bottom closed

Weave in any loose ends on the knitted fabric. To do this, thread your needle with the excess yarn and carefully weave it through the stitches for a few centimetres on the back of the work, making sure that it doesn't show on the right side.

With right sides together, fold the knitted fabric in half widthways, matching up the chevrons at the bottom edge. Using a strand of wool and a blunt-ended needle, neatly sew up the side and bottom edges of the bag using backstitch.

4. Lining

Using your finished, sewn-up knitting as a template, cut two rectangles of lining fabric. They should be the same width as your work and about two – thirds the length. Ours measured 16 cm x 25 cm. Yours may be a wee bit larger or smaller depending on your tension. Fold down the top 1 cm on each piece of lining fabric. Press the fold very well.

fold down 1 cm and press

lining
right side

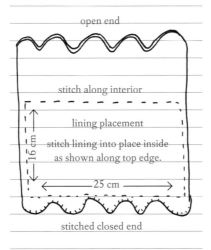

open end

stitch along interior

lining placement

16 cm

stitch lining into place inside as shown along top edge.

25 cm

stitched closed end

With the right sides of the lining pieces facing, stitch them together along the sides and bottom, leaving the pressed edge unsewn and open.
Tuck the lining inside the knitted piece. Use small hand stitches to attach the folded top edge of the lining to the inside of the knitted clutch.

5. Attach the button and press stud

Next, attach one half of the press stud to one side of the inside of the clutch. It should sit between the top edges of the clutch, about 5 cm down from the top edge. Sew it on, keep your stitches small and strong. Attach the other half of the press stud to the other side of the clutch interior, so it meets up perfectly with the first. Press the stud closed and fold the top of the clutch over. Sew the lovely decorative button on the outside of the clutch, as shown in the diagram. Make sure you sew through the outer layer of knitted fabric only (otherwise you won't be able to open the clutch!).

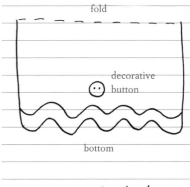

fold

decorative
button

bottom

Now get frocked up and take your clutch out somewhere lovely!

Medal of craftiness

Emma is a capoeira devotee, mum to wonderful Leo and an amazing shoemaker to boot. Her Medal of Craftiness is made with some simple leather tools and a domestic sewing machine with a hardcore needle. It opens up a whole world of crafty possibilities – give it a try.

PROJECT BY: EMMA GREENWOOD
SUITABLE FOR: CAREFUL, PATIENT BEGINNERS
SHOULD TAKE: LESS THAN 1 HOUR

SHOPPING LIST

◇ Kid leather (see Note) – the thinnest and finest that you can find – in two colours or finishes. The finished brooch requires 6 cm × 10 cm (at most) in the main colour and 2 cm × 5 cm in a contrast colour
◇ Brooch back 4 cm wide
◇ Upholstery thread
◇ Silver pen (available from leather suppliers - ballpoint or other pens mark leather permanently, so only use pens specifically designed for leather)
◇ Contact adhesive (such as Kwik Grip)

NOTE

Kid leather is recommended for this project as it has great shine, it cuts cleanly and it has a certain stiffness. Plus the hides are small, so they aren't too expensive! The measurements needed are given above, but you'll need extra to play around with too.

CRAFTY NEEDS

◇ Sewing machine
◇ Chisel-tip or leather needle for domestic sewing machine
◇ Cigarette lighter (or you can use matches, but a lighter gives a steadier, longer-lasting flame)

◇ Cutting mat or thicker piece of leather (to protect the work surface)
◇ Hole punch set, including 1 mm and 3 mm holes
◇ Pointed awl (a special tool for making holes) or needle
◇ Rubber mallet or hammer
◇ Small paintbrush
◇ Zipper foot for domestic machine
◇ Sharp scissors, or craft knife and metal ruler

PATTERN NEEDS

There are two templates for the main brooch piece, but they are used for marking and cutting only one piece of leather. Template A is for marking and cutting the front of the main brooch piece. Template B is for marking and cutting the rear of the main brooch piece. There is also rectangle piece C – you need to cut this out in your contrast colour. This will peep out from under the main piece, through the punched holes.

BEFORE YOU START

Examine the leather for imperfections and stretched areas (these tend to be in the shoulders and hips) and to get a sense of the overall grain. For best results, you need to choose an area that is unmarked and even.

1. Make the brooch

To mark and cut the front of the brooch, place template A on the hide and, using the silver pen, trace around the edges to mark the outer shape of the badge, including the zig-zag bottom edge. Now, using the silver pen, mark a row of 'stitching line' dots as indicated on the template.

Next, you need to mark the brogue holes and fringing position. Do this as follows:

Leaving the template in place, use the awl or needle to carefully prick a line of marks through the template to mark the four top points of the fringing. Please don't pierce right through the hide; you just need to leave small surface marks to act as a guide for later. Also mark small dots above the fringing dots, where you will later punch the brogue holes. Again, just prick the hide rather than piercing it.

Cut out this main badge piece carefully using the scissors or craft knife. Cut the little triangle 'notches' from the bottom of the piece too, as per your template. But don't cut the fringe yet.

2. Cut and punch the brogued part of your brooch

Next, take your leather hole punch, and on a scrap piece of hide work out what size holes you would like. Have a bit of a play around. Be sure to use a cutting mat or thicker piece of leather underneath to protect your work surface.

Once you have chosen the right size, take your main brooch piece, carefully line up the punch with the already pricked hole marks and get punchy!

3. Make the fringe

Make the fringe by ever so carefully snipping from the lower edge to the pinprick marks. Alternatively, use a craft knife and a metal ruler. Neat, neat, neatly you go.

4. Attach the contrasting leather

With the contact adhesive, lightly brush over the back of the brogued (hole-punched) area on the main badge piece and also over the surface of the small contrast piece C. If you use too much glue on the back of the brogueing, it will ooze through the holes and be rather unsightly so

Brooch template

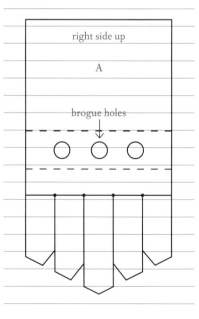

easy does it. With the glue not wet but just tacky, fix the layers together and give a few gentle taps with the hammer to secure.

5. Mark and glue the back of the brooch and attach the brooch back

Trace around the metal brooch back onto the reverse side of the brooch, as we've marked on template B. Brush glue into this marked area and onto the face of the metal brooch back. This is where you can decide which direction you want the brooch back to face when you're fastening it – are you a lefty or a righty? When the glue is tacky, press the brooch back onto the glued area. Take care to keep the brooch back straight, and not at a slight angle; this will affect the way the brooch sits once finished. You don't want it to be wonky.

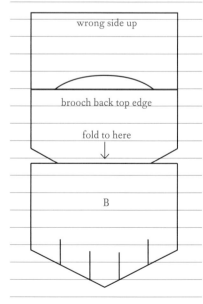

Fold the flap of leather over the brooch back and mark a line with your silver pen where it sits on the reverse side of the work. Apply glue to this entire area – from the line you just marked to the top of the waiting-to-be-folded-over flap. You may need to apply two layers of glue here, as the wrong side of the hide will be a bit thirsty.

Once the glue becomes tacky, fold the leather down neatly to the marked line. Rub over the back surface to fix the layers permanently.

6. Stitch the lines on the front of the brooch

Using the upholstery thread, chisel-tip or leather needle and zipper foot on your domestic sewing machine, stitch along the lines as marked on template A. For a super-neat finish, stop and start one stitch in from the edge of your work on either side. Be sure to stitch very carefully and neatly, as the stitching can't be unpicked without leaving permanent holes in the leather.

Pull loose threads to the back of the work and snip them a few millimetres away from the work. Using the lighter, melt the threads and gently press them onto the back of the piece to finish.

Silver pen marks can be wiped from the leather with a soft cloth. Trim any overhanging edges with scissors.

If the fringing starts to curl over time, wipe the raw side of the leather with a damp cloth and sandwich the fringing between two heavy books.

WEAR YOUR medal with PRIDE!

Granny squares for the very beginner

I learnt to crochet at Brown Owls, our craft club, and after a couple of weeks of undoing and tears – I finally got it worked out! I'm hooked now. There's no one pattern for granny squares, or one 'right' way of doing them. I think I've combined various methods to come up with my renegade square pattern. Give it a try!

PROJECT BY: PIP LINCOLNE

SUITABLE FOR: BEGINNERS

SHOULD TAKE: 40 MINUTES OR SO FOR THE FIRST FEW SQUARES – LESS AS YOU GET THE HANG OF IT.

SHOPPING LIST

◇ One 5.5 mm crochet hook
(metal, please, for extra slipperiness)
◇ A few balls of 8-ply yarn in colours you like. They can be complimentary or they can clash – whatever you like. It's nice to use lots of different colours, I think. (And this is a great way to use up odds and ends, too!)

CRAFTY NEEDS

◇ Scissors
◇ Pencil, to mark where you are up to on the page as you go
◇ Eraser, to rub out the marks so you don't spoil this book

BEFORE YOU START

If you are new to crochet, see page 130. We're learning three crochet basics – chain stitch, treble stitch and slip stitch. Consult our handy diagrams to learn how!

NOTE

Mark your steps off with a pencil as you go to keep your place. It's okay to get a bit cross at first – but I promise you that once you've got this, you'll be doing it like a pro, with one eye on the telly and the other on the hooking! Go slowly and master each stage before moving on to the next. If you make a mistake, just pull it undone and start again – no sweat!

1. Lay the foundation for your square by making the circular centre

Imagine it – the centre of a granny square is a circle! Make a slipknot and thread your hook through it. See the 'How to make a slipknot' diagram on page 130.

Pull your yarn so that it's taut, but not super-tight – you need to be able to get the hook in and out of your stitches easily.

◇ Make six chain stitches – this will give you a nice circle to crochet in and out of later. See How to Crochet on page 130.

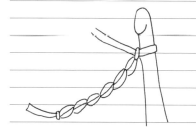

◇ Join the chain stitches with a slip stitch, thus making a circle or ring. To do this, poke your hook (which has one loop on it at present) through the first 'chain' stitch of the six you just made – you'll now have two loops on the hook.

◇ Slip the top loop through the bottom loop. To do this, pull the yarn loop nearest the top part of your hook through and under the second (bottom) loop – thus joining the ends of your chain. You should only have one loop on the hook now. Pull the chain-stitch circle into shape and poke your pinky through the centre to help define it better Excellent! You made a crochet ring! Let's move on.

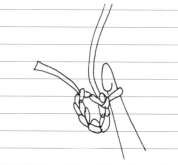

2. Make your first 'round'

◇ Make three chain stitches. This will, in effect, lift your yarn and hook up to the height of the next 'round' of your granny square. Make sure your crochet ring is still nice and circular. If it's not, poke it with your finger to get it back into shape.
◇ Here's where we start our 'treble' stitch. See How to Crochet on page 130.

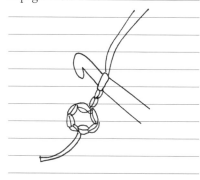

◇ Putting the hook through the centre of the crochet ring, make two treble stitches, hooking in and out of the central ring each time you treble.
◇ It's important to note that the chain of three you just worked makes the first part of this first crochet cluster – the chains count as one stitch. (This only happens at the beginning of a round; everywhere else the 'clusters' are made up of *three* treble stitches.)

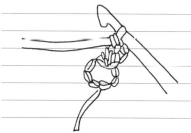

◇ Now you've made your first cluster of stitches. (We'll be making four clusters in total.)
◇ Now make two chain stitches to create the gap between the clusters.

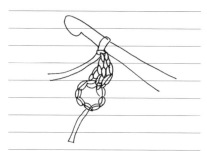

◇ Treble three stitches through the centre ring.

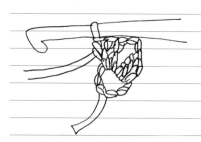

◇ Chain two more stitches.

◇ Treble three stitches again, into the centre ring.

◇ Chain two more.

◇ Treble three stitches once again into the centre ring.

Now you'll have four clusters of three treble stitches, with gaps in between them.

◇ Chain one more stitch.

◇ Slip stitch it all together. To do this, poke your hook into the top edge of the 'treble' cluster you are next to. This will form the link or join and keep things nice and even. You have completed a round!

3. Round two, and how to change colour

◇ Take the next colour yarn you want to crochet with.

◇ Make a slip knot with your fingers and slip it onto the hook. Yep, it already has a loop of the first colour on it. That's okay. You want *both* coloured loops on there at first.

◇ Now, you're going to hold both threads of yarn nice and firmly and hook the *new* colour under the *first* colour. Keep all your threads tight.

◇ Next, with your new colour, make three chain stitches, taking you up to the top of your next round. Now you can leave the previous coloured

yarn behind and use the new colour to crochet with. We can stitch your ends in later. Just cut a tail about 8 cm long on the first coloured yarn. You're onto your new colour!

◇ Flip your work over so you're working on the other side.

◇ Treble two stitches into the hole or 'gap' at the bottom left of your chain. If you're thinking it's part of your previous round, you are right!

◇ Now Chain 2.

◇ Treble 3 into the same gap that you just trebled into. You've made a corner!

◇ Chain 1.

You're about to treble into the next gap (in the *previous* round). It's over to the left. Find that gap and off we go …

◇ Treble 3 into the gap (this is the start of your corner).

◇ Chain 2.

◇ Treble 3 into the same gap (this is the end of your corner).

◇ Chain 1 and treble into the *next* gap (not the one you just trebled into) – you'll find it over to the left (in the round below) and …

◇ Treble 3 into this next gap.

◇ Chain 2.

◇ Treble 3 into this same gap – you've made another corner!

◇ Chain 1 and move over to the *next* gap (it's to the left in the previous round).

◇ Treble 3 into this new 'gap'.

◇ Chain 2.

◇ Treble 3 into the same gap (another corner!).

To finish the square off,

◇ Chain 1 and slip stitch (as you did at the end of the previous round) to join to the treble cluster next door.

4. Notice your crochet building blocks

Stop and have a look at what we have just done. You can see that your granny square is taking shape. Notice that the corners are made up of a cluster of three treble stitches, then two chain stitches, then another three treble stitches. And that chain stitch joins the clusters that run along the sides of your square. Using this sort of foundation, you can make your 'rounds' as big as you like. Just keep the corners the same as we've described – and then each little cluster of trebles along the sides of your square is joined by only one chain stitch. Note that you need to work along the side trebling into the gaps of the previous round. Let's do one more together.

5. Another round!

◇ Chain up 3. Flip your work and start working into the bottom left gap of the previous round, where you started your chain. You need to:
◇ Treble 2.
◇ Chain 1 – this is the side cluster of this round.
Reach across to the next left gap (in the previous round) and
◇ Treble 3 into that gap.
◇ Chain 2.
◇ Treble 3 into the same gap – you just made a corner of your new round!
◇ Chain 1.
Reach across to the next left gap (in the previous round, like we did before).
◇ Treble 3.
◇ Chain 1 – that's another side for your round.
Reach across to the next left gap in your work.
◇ Treble 3 into that gap.
◇ Chain 2.
◇ Treble 3 into the same gap – that's a corner!
◇ Chain 1.
As before, reach across to the next left gap in the previous round of your work.
◇ Treble 3.
◇ Chain 1 – there's the side cluster.
Find your next left gap in the previous round.
◇ Treble 3 into that gap.
◇ Chain 2.
◇ Treble 3 into the same gap.
Another corner!
And continue, checking your work as you go …
◇ Chain 1.
◇ Treble 3.

◇ Chain 1 – fourth side!
◇ Treble 3.
◇ Chain 2.
◇ Treble 3 – last corner!
◇ Chain 1 and slip stitch to join to the previous cluster.

You can continue on like this to build as many rounds as you like. Just remember that the corners need two chain stitches between the treble clusters, but the sides only need one chain stitch between each cluster. Be sure to double-check that you are trebling into the right gap as you go!

Note: If you've got a nanna or a clever elderly neighbour handy, it's lovely to ask her about her crochet skills – what better way to make a crafty connection?! Failing that, youtube.com is a ready friend with crochet video tutorials.

6. Some little rules for my squares:

The centre of the square is 6 Chain to form a loop – that makes a nice big loop to work into for beginners. Start each new round by chaining up 3 and trebling 2.
A corner is 3 Treble, 2 Chain, 3 Treble. Clusters of 3 Treble along the sides are joined by 1 Chain.
When finishing off the square, slip stitch with only one chain to keep the square tight and neat.

7. To weave in or finish off your loose ends:

Take your yarn needle and thread your the tail of the yarn through it. Now, working on the wrong (worst!) side of your square, carefully weave the needle under the row of crochet stitches nearest to your finished end. Weave your needle under for about 5 cm.

Pull the needle and yarn through and gently tug until firm. Now, skipping the last two (just-threaded-under stitches), push your needle back in the opposite direction through the same stitches, again under the stitches on the wrong side of your work.

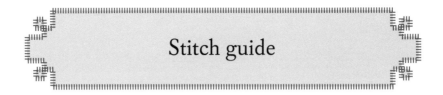

Stitch guide

I like stitching. It's kind of like colouring in with a needle and thread.
And it's extremely useful for sewing up toys whose stuffing may otherwise run amok.
This guide will help you get stitched up in a whole host of ways. It will also make people
thrust their mending at you, so keep it under the table (unless you like mending).

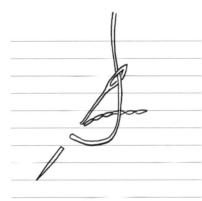

Backstitch

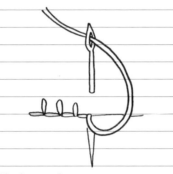

Blanket stitch

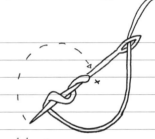

French knot

Backstitch is a really neat, easy stitch.
It's a simple way to outline your
chosen design with a solid line.
You need to keep your stitches the
same length for best results.
To backstitch, stitch one stitch – then
bring the needle up through the fabric
a stitch length away from the previous
stitch. Now take your needle back
down into the end of the previous
stitch. Now off you go again – up a
stitch length away from that stitch –
and back down into the end of the
previous. You're doing the backstitch!

Blanket stitch is fantastic for finishing
edges and stitching around curves in
a decorative way. Bring your needle
up through the fabric and then push
it through the top of your work about
0.5 cm diagonally opposite your entry
point, and then back up another 0.5 cm
from this point – level with your
original entry point. Pull your floss
through, looping your thread under
your needle to form a blanket stitch.

A seemingly tricky stitch, but it's
simple when you know how!
Bring your threaded and knotted
needle up through to the top of your
work. Pull the floss right through
firmly. Lay your needle across the
spot right next to where your thread
just came through. Now wrap the floss
around the needle 3 or 4 times at the
pointy end, still keeping your thread
tight and your needle in place. This
wound-around floss will form most
of your French knot. Next, carefully
pull the wrapped around thread down
to the eye-end of the needle – away
from the pointy end. Using your
thumb, keep guiding the wrapped-
around thread back down and off the
threaded end of the needle until it
touches the fabric. It's nearly a knot.
Now make a tiny stitch where the
wrapped knot of thread 'landed' to
secure and finish your knot.

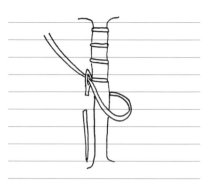

Ladder stitch

Ladder Stitch looks like a little ladder, doesn't it? It's a way of joining fabric almost invisibly at each edge – and for sewing openings closed neatly. The idea is to stitch in a ladder-like formation, stitching parallel lines across the join or opening. Keep your stitches loose, but even, and when complete, pull the thread nice and tight. Knot off to secure.

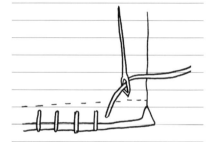

Overcast stitch

Overcast stitch involves stitching over the edges of the fabric to neaten a raw edge and prevent fraying. You just need to make a nice, even over and over stitch through both edges of your fabric as shown. Keep your stitches nice and small too, for best results.

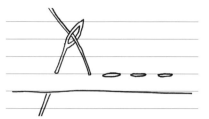

Running stitch

A lovely naïve under and over stitch you may have learnt in kindergarten! If not, here's how. Make a stitch by pushing the needle up from under your work, then back down a nice stitch length away, then leave a stitch-length gap and come up again with your needle, and then back down – continuing on with an even, 'gappy' stitch.

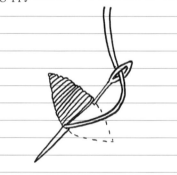

Satin stitch

A great stitch for filling in areas that need 'colouring in'. Satin stitch is long, straight, fine stitches with a hand-drawn or transferred outline. Stitches are kept very close beside each other – how sweet!

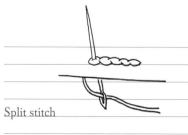

Split stitch

Split stitch is the Splitsville sister of backstitch. Another good stitch for outlining designs – it looks like a little chain. To make a Split stitch, knot your floss and make one short first stitch – up through your work and then down into the fabric – voila. One short stitch. Now, push your needle back up through the centre of this first short stitch, thus splitting the stitch. Now, back down into your work an even stitch length away from the last stitch – now 'split' back up through the middle of the previous stitch – thus each new stitch splits the last. Continue on in this manner.

Topstitch

Topstitch involves finishing a sewn piece by stitching a line of regular old straight stitches (at the required seam allowance). It provides a nice finish and can be done by hand or by machine.

Whip stitch

A simple over and over stitch that can be used to make a hem – or close an opening. Keep stitches small and even for best results and knot off securely at the end, stitching a couple of small extra-tight stitches for security.

How to crochet

My life changed when I learnt to crochet. It's true. I spent weeks trying to learn with sympathetic family members telling me to give it up. Tears flowed, rude words were uttered, and that was just them. I was a determined nutcase, and I would not be beaten. In the end I got there, and now I speak the language. You should learn too, so we can speak crochet together.

Slip knot

The slip knot is the very first stitch you slip onto your crochet hook! Here's how to slip!

◇ Place the yarn over your finger like so. Be sure you have plenty of excess.

◇ Wrap the excess yarn around your fingertip two more times.

◇ Now pull Loop A up and over Loop B as shown.

A   B

◇ Next, you need to pull Loop B up and over Loop A.

A   B

◇ Now grab the Back Loop and pull it up and off your finger – you'll be dragging the other loop after it, thus making a slip knot.

back loop
↓

◇ Voila!

Simple slipstitch

The slipstitch (not to be confused with the slip knot!) is used in the Morris the Sensitive Panda project (page 20). You can also use it to make your first foundation chain into a loop when making a granny square (page 122).

With the loop still on your hook, push the hook through the last stitch as specified. Hook your yarn over and pull this new loop through to the front of your work and through bottom two loops on your hook.

Chain stitch

Chain stitch is often the foundation for crochet projects. It's so easy to do too!

◇ Put your slip knot onto the hook – we'll call it Loop A.

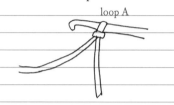

loop A

◇ Wrap your yarn around the hook like so:

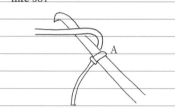

A

◇ Hook the just wrapped around yarn B under Loop A to make your very first chain.

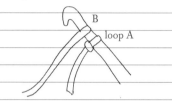

B

loop A

◇ It should look a bit like this:

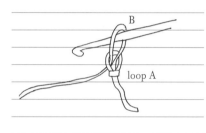

B

loop A

◇ Make another chain. Wrap your yarn around, then hook yarn C under Loop B as shown:

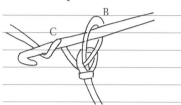

B

C

◇ You've made another chain – hurrah!

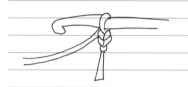

◇ Continue on in this manner – making as many chain stitches as you need to.

Double crochet (referred to as single crochet in the US)

◇ With the loop on your hook, push your hook into the front of the second chain stitch from your hook. You don't count the stitch on your hook, though. Start on the next one.

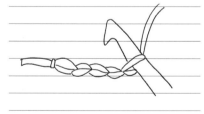

◇ With your hook still pushed through that stitch, hook your yarn and pull it back through to the front of your work. You should now have two loops on the hook.

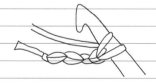

◇ Hook your yarn again and pull this hooked yarn under the bottom two loops on your hook.

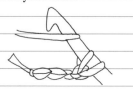

◇ You should now have one loop on your hook again.

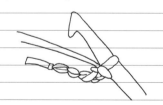

◇ Hook into the next chain across and repeat.
◇ When you reach the end of a row, turn your work around, chain up one and continue on.

Treble crochet (referred to as double crochet in the US)

I like treble, because it's a vital stitch in the world of granny squaring! When you crochet a granny square, you treble these stitches in and out of a foundation circle or loop. But crochet is not just about grannies, is it? You can also treble stitch into a length of chain stitch for less granny-type projects.

◇ With the loop on your hook push your hook through your chosen stitch (or ring or gap, depending on your project). For many projects this will be the third chain stitch from the hook. But, if you're making a granny square, then you should hook into the 'gap or ring' as detailed in your instructions.

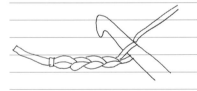

◇ With the hook still pushed through, hook your yarn and pull it back through to the front of your work.

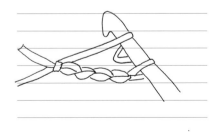

◇ Now you need to hook your yarn around yet again. You'll now have four loops on your hook.

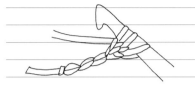

◇ Next, pull the loop near the hooky tip under and through the middle two loops – leaving you with only two loops on your hook (not four anymore).

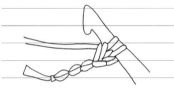

◇ Now hook your yarn around again and pull it through the bottom two loops. You should now have only one loop on your hook. Yippee!

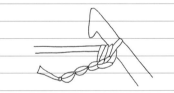

◇ Repeat as detailed in your instructions.

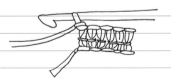

Note: If you're crocheting a row rather than a granny square – when you get to the end of your row, turn your work around. Chain stitch up three and continue on.

Crochet abbreviations and terms

These vary dramatically. This book uses the UK, Australian and international terminology.

Abbreviation	UK, Australian and International term
ch	chain
sl st	slip stitch
dc	double crochet *(referred to as single crochet in the US)*
tr	treble *(referred to as double crochet in the US)*
st(s)	stitches
dec 1	decrease 1
inc 1	increase 1

Note on Hooks

There are recommended hook sizes for various ply yarns.
Consult your yarn store for advice – as it really does make a huge different to the finished size and result of your project.

Note on Yarn

Always use the yarn thickness (ply) recommended – many projects simply won't work if you use the wrong ply although experienced crocheters can often juggle yarns and hooks and gauge and make it work. That could be you some day.

How to knit

My lovely Nanna taught me to knit, and so ensued a rather large amount of doll's blankets (which were really abandoned, half-knitted scarves). I was only eight then and now I can actually knit a whole scarf. I can even cast on and cast off. Great progress, I say! Knitting is all about practice. So practice and knit you will!

Knitting tips

Your pattern will tell you which needles and yarn to use, and the recommended needle size also appears on the label of your yarn. If in doubt, ask your friendly yarn retailer.

Holding the needles and yarn

Don't worry if you're all fingers and thumbs to start off with – those fingers and thumbs will be your very favourite friends once you get the hang of this.

◇ There are lots of ways to hold your needles, but why don't you try holding the right needle in the right hand just like a pencil? Hold the left needle lightly at the top, using your thumb and index finger to control it. Make sure you are comfy and relaxed. Be sure that your yarn is in the right place (at the front or the back of your work – according to the stitch you are knitting and that you're not knitting with the 'tail' of your yarn. Remember to take it slow when you are learning. Dropped stitches are not fun!

HINT
leftover wool
is great for
granny squares

Dye lots

Each ball of yarn comes from a particular dye lot. If you're using more then one ball of yarn for a project, be sure they are all from the same dye lot. The dye lot details appear on the label of the yarn. That way you can be sure that all your yarn matches exactly.

Tension

Tension is not a bad thing in knitting. It's a really useful thing. Some patterns will recommend you knit a square to work out whether your tension is tight or loose – which will mean your project might end up bigger or smaller then intended. Check your pattern – it will have a little note about how many stitches should fit into an inch (or cm). Measure your work and adjust your knitting accordingly if it's too small, loosen up a bit or too big, tighten up those stitches!

Have a look on the internet for other how-to resources, it is full of how-to-knit videos, just in case you need to see all this in action. Go search, it's super-helpful.

How to cast on

Make a slip knot.

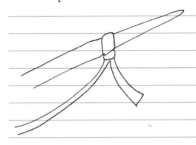

Poke the right hand knitting needle into the slip knot (you should poke from front to back to make an "X" with your needles). Now wrap the yarn (not the tail of the yarn) over the point of the right hand needle. You should wrap the yarn by curling it around the front of the needle and then around to to the back.

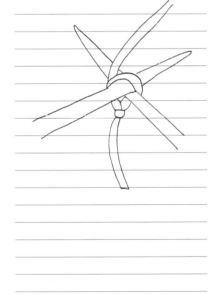

Keep the yarn pulled fairly tight in your right hand. Carefully sliding the needle down, poke the tip of your right hand needle down and through the stitch on the left hand needle. You should now have two loops - one on each needle.

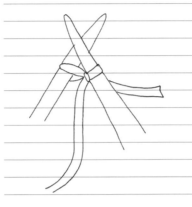

Poke the left hand needle into the loop that's on the right hand needle and transfer this loop over to the left one. Pull your yarn taut. That's a stitch cast on! You'll have two on your left needle now.

Let's make another stitch! Poke the right hand needle into the top loop on the left. We're going to do it all again! Wrap the yarn around the right hand needle as before (from front to back). Then, as before, poke the tip of the right hand needle down and through the top stitch on the left hand needle. You'll now have two stitches on the left needle and one on the right. Transfer this right loop/stitch over to the left hand needle to join the other 'cast-on' stitches. Continue on like this until the required number of stitches is 'cast-on'.

Basic knit stitch

A bumpy stitch that my nan calls 'plain' stitch. It's also referred to as 'garter stitch'.

Start with your cast on stitches on the left needle. The strand of yarn leading to the ball of yarn should be at the back of your work. Now insert the right needle into the top stitch on the left needle as shown. The right needle needs to be tucked in behind the left one to form an 'X' – the left needle is at the front with it's little row of 'cast on' stitches. See?

Wrap the yarn around the right needle (which should still be tucked behind and at the rear of the left one) over the point of the right hand needle. Keep the yarn fairly tight.

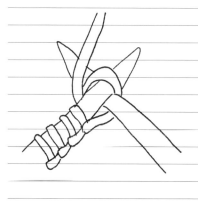

Slide the right hand needle downwards carefully and poke the point of the right hand needle down and under the top stitch on the left needle. Now you just slip the top stitch on the left needle off the left needle. There you go, you knitted a stitch. Hurrah!

Basic purl stitch

For purl stitch, start with your cast on stitches on the left needle (in your left hand). The yarn attached to the ball should be at the front of your work. Now insert the right needle into the top stitch on the left needle as shown. The right needle should to be at the front. (The left needle tucked behind at the rear to form an 'X'. It's kind of the opposite to the basic knit stitch.)

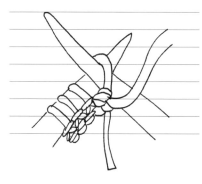

Wrap the yarn over the front and then around under the tip of the right needle to create a loop. Excellent.

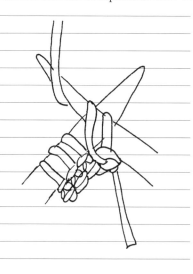

Carefully slide the right hand needle downwards and under the left hand needle. Slip the top loop off the left hand needle to complete the stitch. Awesome, you purled!

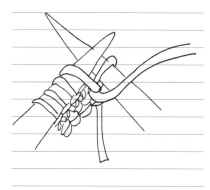

How to bind off or cast off

This is how you finish off your knitting when you are at the last row. It creates a nice finished seam and stops your knitting from unravelling.

Knit the first two stitches using the basic knit stitch. How funny, but you need two stitches on your right needle to cast off one stitch. You will now have your nearly finished work on the left needle and two stitches on the right needle.

Using either the tip of the left needle, if you are dextrous, or your fingers if you are not, pull the bottom loop up and over the top loop. Now you should have only one stitch on the right needle.

Knit the next stitch (from the left needle with your nearly finished work on it). Now again pull the bottom loop up and over the top loop and off the needle. Continue on like this until you have bound off all but one stitch.

Thread the 'tail' of the yarn through this last stitch and tie off securely. Voila!

Pink lamingtons

Pink lamingtons. They're a bit cuter then a regular lamington, aren't they?
Put them side-by-side on a pretty plate and I know you'll go for the pink one every time
because they're a bit unusual and it's a long time between pink lamingtons, isn't it?
I don't like jam or cream in mine. If you do, then you can do that. But I don't.

SHOPPING LIST

1 packet raspberry jelly crystals
1¼ cups boiling water
1 plain sponge cake – rectangular is best
3 cups desiccated coconut

HOW TO MAKE IT

Mix the jelly crystals with the boiling water and stir until the crystals dissolve. Put into the fridge in a wide dish (for ease of dipping), until starting to set a bit Keep a close eye on the jelly.

Cut your cake into squares, perhaps huge, perhaps tiny! Do it the way you like.

Tip coconut onto a tray or wide dish of some kind, ready for rolling the lamingtons.

When your jelly is ready, dip the plain cake into the nearly set jelly until coated on all sides.

Roll in the coconut until completely covered.

Enjoy with a nice cup of Earl Grey tea and a few episodes of 'That Girl' with Marlo Thomas.

Contributors

Allison Jones
Teeny-tiny goody-two-shoes (page 12)
www.the-lark.blogspot.com

Lara Cameron
Fabric clock (page 16)
www.kirinote.blogspot.com

Jess McCaughey
Morris the sensitive panda (page 20)
www.teddybearswednesday.blogspot.com

Kristen Doran
Drawstring case (page 24)
www.cheekybeaks.blogspot.com

Alison Brookbanks
Mini quilt (page 30)
www.sixandahalfstitches.typepad.com

Claire Robertson
Softie wheat-bag friend (page 34)
www.loobylu.com

Erin Lewis
Phoney flowers (page 38)
www.whatabouthoney.com

Carly Schwerdt
Moopy's lovely notebook cover (page 44)
www.neststudio.typepad.com

Gemma Jones
Hand-printed friendship hankies (page 48)
www.gemmajones.net

Nichola Prested
Cutest ever baby knickers (page 52)
www.nikkishell.com

Fliss Dodd
Udderly lovely cow (page 56)
www.udder.typepad.com

Angela White
Shopping bag keep-safe (page 62)
www.threebuttons.blogspot.com

Kara Smith
Cute-as-a button vintage clutch (page 66)
www.karasmith.com.au

Suzie Fry
Butterfly Evelyn (page 70)
www.soozs.blogspot.com

Jennie McClelland
Super-cute tote (page 74)
www.ednaalicemay.com.au

Anna Laura Blandford
Custom-designed felt brooch (page 78)
www.annalauraart.blogspot.com

Kate Henderson
Really useful fabric roll (page 82)
www.neverenoughhours.blogspot.com

Tiel Seivl-Keevers
Flower and bird coasters (page 86)
www.tsktsk.typepad.com

Nanette Louchart-Fletcher
Made-to-measure vintage obi and
skirt/halter top (page 90)
www.rummage.typepad.com

Jhoanna Monte Aranez
Zing the polite cat (page 96)
www.oneredrobin.com

Shannon Lamden
Yoga pants for happy babies (page 100)
www.auntycookie.com

Marianne Horton
Ephemera mobile (page 104)
www.applehead.typepad.com

Leah Chapman
Fabric backgammon board (page 110)
www.hyena-in-petticoats.blogspot.com

Kylie Robson
Chevron clutch (page 114)
www.kgirlknits.blogspot.com

Emma Greenwood
Medal of craftiness (page 118)
www.apronsandhammers.blogspot.com

Pip Lincolne
Granny squares for the very
beginner (page 122)
www.meetmeatmikes.com

Acknowledgements

Firstly – a huge thank you to all the crafters featured in this book –
who gave their time and expertise with grace and humour.
You are all very clever, I reckon.

Extra super dooper special thanks to the following ace people. I couldn't have done it without you.
My family: my parents, my nanna, my Uncle Ken, my little sister, my other nanna and my brother too.
My boyfriend, Cameron Steel and the sweetest, smartest kids ever, Max and Ari and Rin.
Dave Steel for his constant strength, support and super-niceness and
Betty Steel – seamstress extraordinaire (just the Steels in general, actually).

My lovely friends and helpers:
Kirsty, Gemma, Brooke, Angela, Molly, Hollie, Souraya, Aimee, Emma, Vic, Jess and Allison.

Frankie, Fran Atkinson, Michigirl, David and Dur-e, Nellie and Amy Prior.

All the lovely Brown Owls and readers of my blog and visitors to Mike's.

Lovely Sim and handsome Tim for doing a great job with this book.

Mary and Ellie for being so enthusiastic and steering me in the right direction.

Serap and Olive for modelling so prettily.

Lucky, Snoopy, Mike and Nibbles (RIP).

Thank you to Mitch too.

Finally for paving a really terrific crafty path for people like me to follow,
I would like to thank Amy Karol, Loobylu, Amy Butler, Alicia Paulson, Sublime Stitching, Craftzine and Whipup.

Oh.. and also to Richard Stubbs. Ha ha! Thank you!